Once in Broome

SALLY BIN DEMIN
with Karen Atkinson

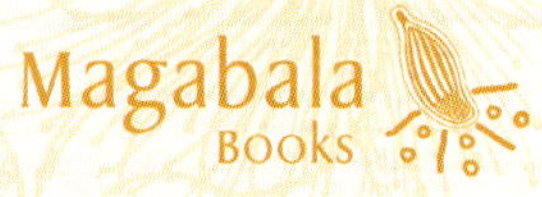

First published in 2007, reprinted 2012, 2017
Magabala Books Aboriginal Corporation, Broome, Western Australia
Website: www.magabala.com Email: sales@magabala.com

Magabala Books receives financial assistance from the Commonwealth Government through the Australia Council, its arts advisory body. The State of Western Australia has made an investment in this project through the Department of Culture and the Arts in association with Lotterywest. Magabala Books would like to acknowledge the generous support of the Shire of Broome, Western Australia.

Designed by Jo Hunt
Printed in China at Everbest Printing Company

National Library of Australia
Cataloguing-in-Publication
Bin Demin, Sally (Ursula Selina), 1942- .
Once in Broome...

ISBN 9781921248061
1. Bin Demin, Sally (Ursula Selina), 1942- . 2. Women artists, Aboriginal Australian - Western Australia - Broome - Biography.
3. Art, Aboriginal Australian - Western Australia - Broome.
I. Title.

709.2

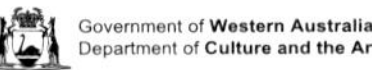

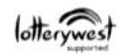

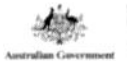
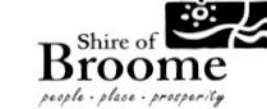

To the memory of my mother, Barbara, and Aunty Bella and Simeon, who have inspired me throughout my life.
To my children, Anthea and Johari, and to my grandchildren and future generations.

Acknowledgements

Thanks to Karen Atkinson who first encouraged me to tell my story. Karen and I spent many hours talking and driving around town revisiting my childhood places and showing her what 'used to be there'. It was her friendship and skill to 'ask the right questions' that shaped the publication of this book.

Special thanks to my partner, Ahmat Bin Fadal, for his understanding and for helping with the Malay language words. Thanks to my sister, Pearl Hamaguchi, for providing photographs from her private collection, and to Yaja Hadrys for the photographs of my silk paintings. Thanks also to Doris Edgar and Diane Appleby for their advice on Yawuru words, and to Joyce Hudson and Carol Tang Wei for their support on language matters.

My family and friends were very patient while I worked on this book. Sometimes they jogged my memory with their casual remarks, and at other times they made a point of reminding me of something that needed to be included. For their support and love, thank you.

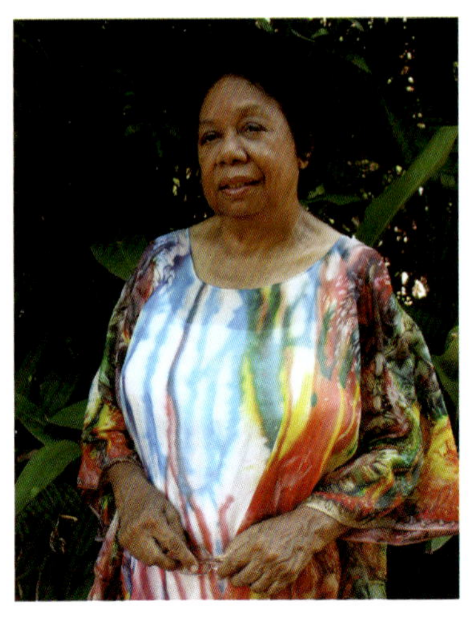

I have written this book for my grandchildren, and future generations, in the hope that it may give them understanding about their heritage, and help them to value what has gone before them. I am a Broome woman, a wife, a mother, and a grandmother. As I have grown older, I have come to realise how special it was to be a child growing up in Broome in the 1940s and 1950s.

I was one of the 'after the war' kids and we always say that we had the best of Broome. Of course, this may be a false perception because children before the war were even more isolated and free from the influences of the rest of Australia.

Even so, the lifestyle we led was unique, embedded as it was in the traditions of so many cultures. Our relationships with family and friends were caring, and the bonds we formed with our countrymen were strong and abiding. We depended on each other and everybody worked hard. Even as children we had clear boundaries and we knew what was expected of us. We also knew how to have fun — our lives were carefree and we lived in the moment with little worry for the future.

The environment was pristine. Today, working as an artist, the visions of my childhood are reflected in the form and colour of my work. The world I grew up in was a picture, from the Ming blue of the ocean to the soft aqua closer to shore, and from the radiant light of sunset to the brilliant red of the cliffs. The shapes I draw are the neverending trails of *omong omong* (hermit crabs) in the sand, the flash of silvery *walga walga* (salmon) leaping through the water, mangoes hanging from a branch and frangipani spilling on the ground.

This is the story of my childhood. There are many such stories, but I can only tell mine, as seen through my eyes. I was 'grown up' in a culture that values stories above most else, where the telling of stories was entertainment and the lifeblood connecting us to our identity and our heritage. My story isn't one with a beginning or an end. I am descended from the Jaru people of the East Kimberley and I also have Asian blood in my veins — our stories are told over and over so that we know them well. Sometimes I may repeat myself, sometimes the memories lead me off into different directions and I follow.

Sally Bin Demin

This book contains names and photographs of people who have passed away, which may cause sadness to some people.

The town of Broome and its environs is home to the Yawuru and Djugun Aboriginal people. Since the 1880s, the town has evolved with a rich multicultural history unlike any other place in Australia. During the heyday of the pearling years, hundreds of luggers worked out of Roebuck Bay, and the pearl shell industry attracted workers from Asian shores and beyond. By the time Sally Bin Demin was growing up, after the Second World War, words from many other languages had found their way into the Broome vernacular. Sometimes their origins are not clear. In *Once in Broome*, words other than English are in italics and, if necessary, are followed by an English translation.

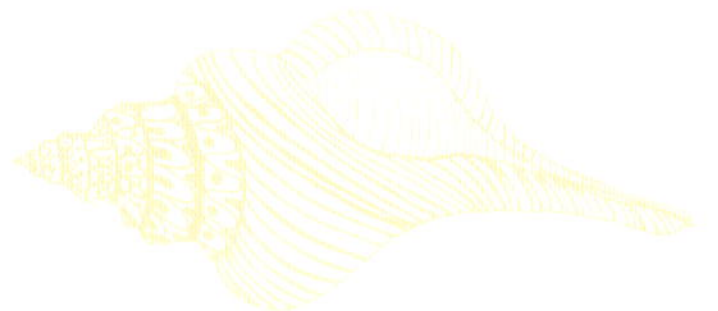

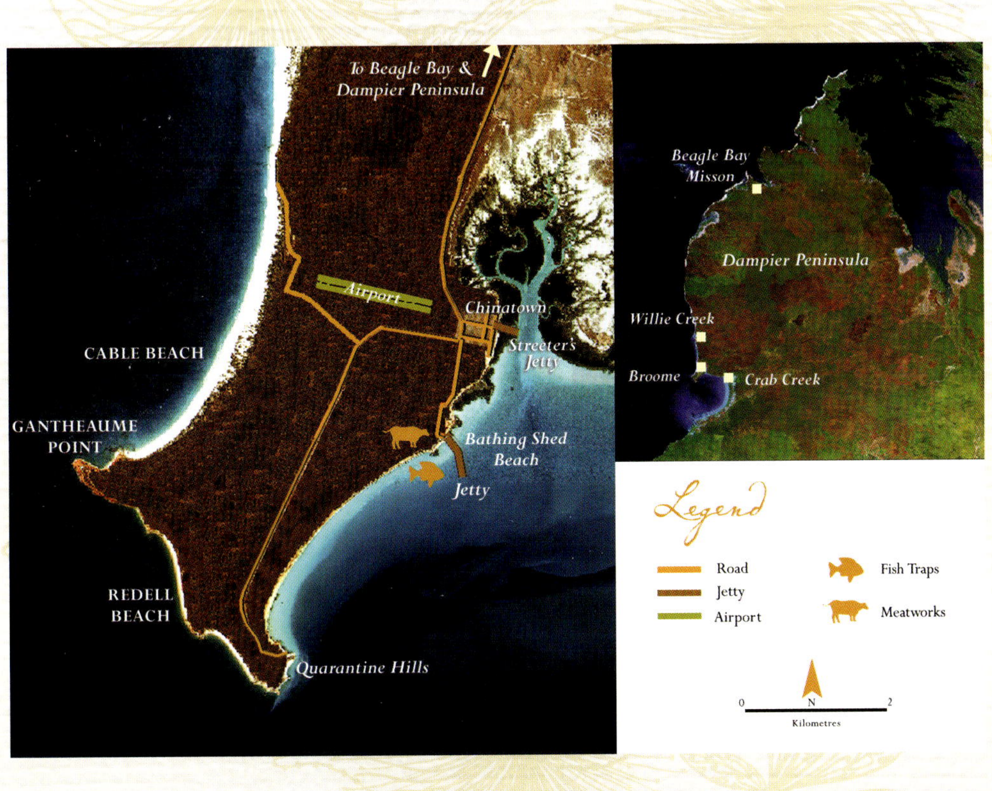
To Beagle Bay &
Dampier Peninsula
Airport
Chinatown
Streeter's
Jetty
CABLE BEACH
GANTHEAUME
POINT
Bathing Shed
Beach
Jetty
REDELL
BEACH
Quarantine Hills
Beagle Bay
Misson
Dampier Peninsula
Willie Creek
Broome
Crab Creek
Legend
Road
Jetty
Airport
Fish Traps
Meatworks
0
N
2
Kilometres

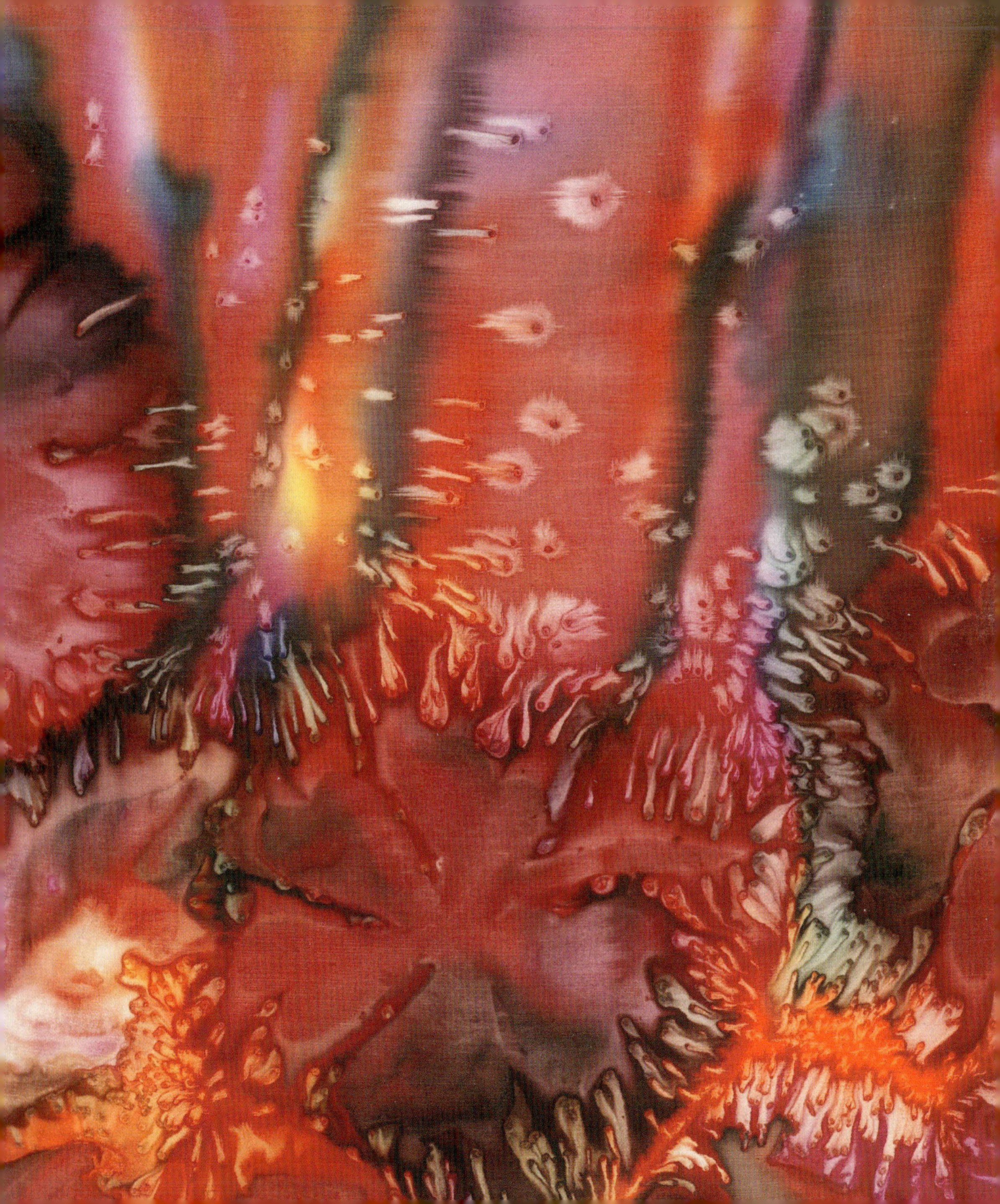

Dark clouds were forming over Broome, and the damp heat clung to the women as they gathered their belongings. They lifted the children onto the back of the truck before clambering up and sitting beside them. There was a goat tied to the back railing to provide milk for the children.

It was early March, 1942, and as the Japanese planes flew closer, this small group of evacuees was the last to leave Broome. Their menfolk didn't journey to Beagle Bay. Some were in the Home Guards and some were in the army. It was war and all the Japanese living in Broome — divers, businessmen, and their families — were taken to Melbourne and interned.

I was eight months in my mother's tummy and kicking out at my twin brother as we headed north up the Dampier Peninsula towards the Catholic mission at Beagle Bay. Mum was travelling with my two-year-old sister, Pearl, and four other families. Uncle Ben Mathews drove the truck slowly over the rough dirt road, and they headed across the marsh near Willie Creek. The truck needed fixing, and it was here that the group of women decided to stop for the night. There was a little soak nearby where someone years ago had planted a beautiful date palm.

The Japanese planes were chasing the Dutch flying boats and were moving quickly overhead. The little group sat quietly glancing up at the darkening sky. The mozzies were in plague numbers, and there was a mosquito net to cover the children. The women were being eaten alive. When dawn finally appeared, they climbed back onto the truck and jolted and bounced all the way to Beagle Bay.

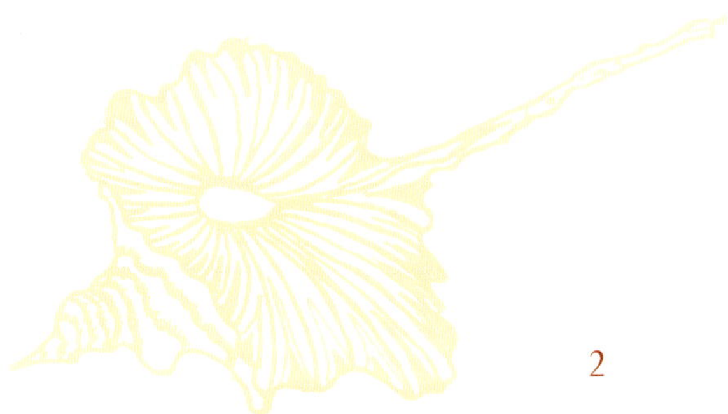

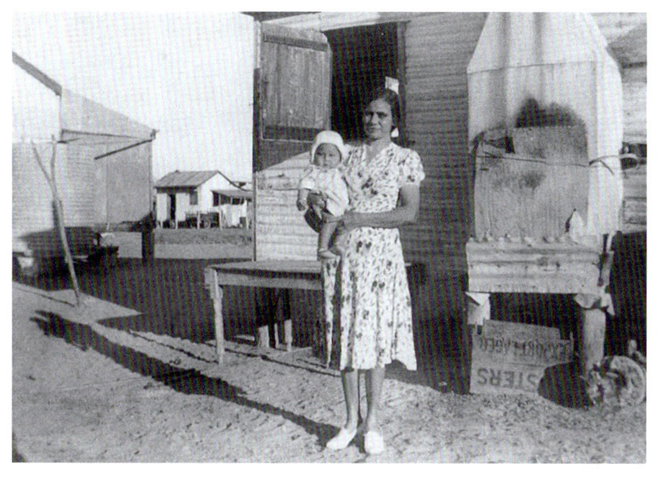

Mum with Pearl, at the back of our house on the foreshore, Short Street, Broome, 1940.

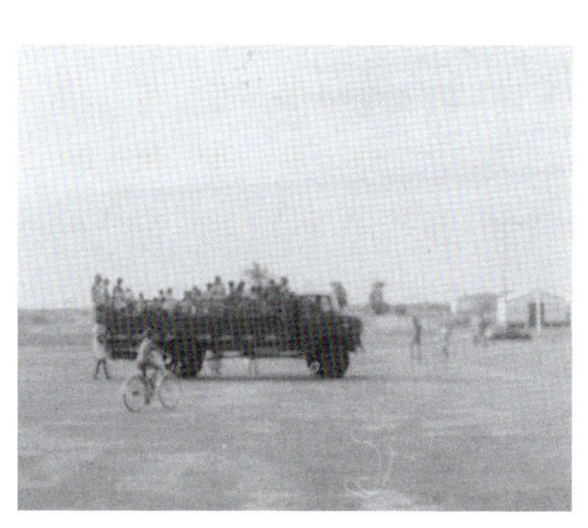

The Beagle Bay mission truck in Chinatown.

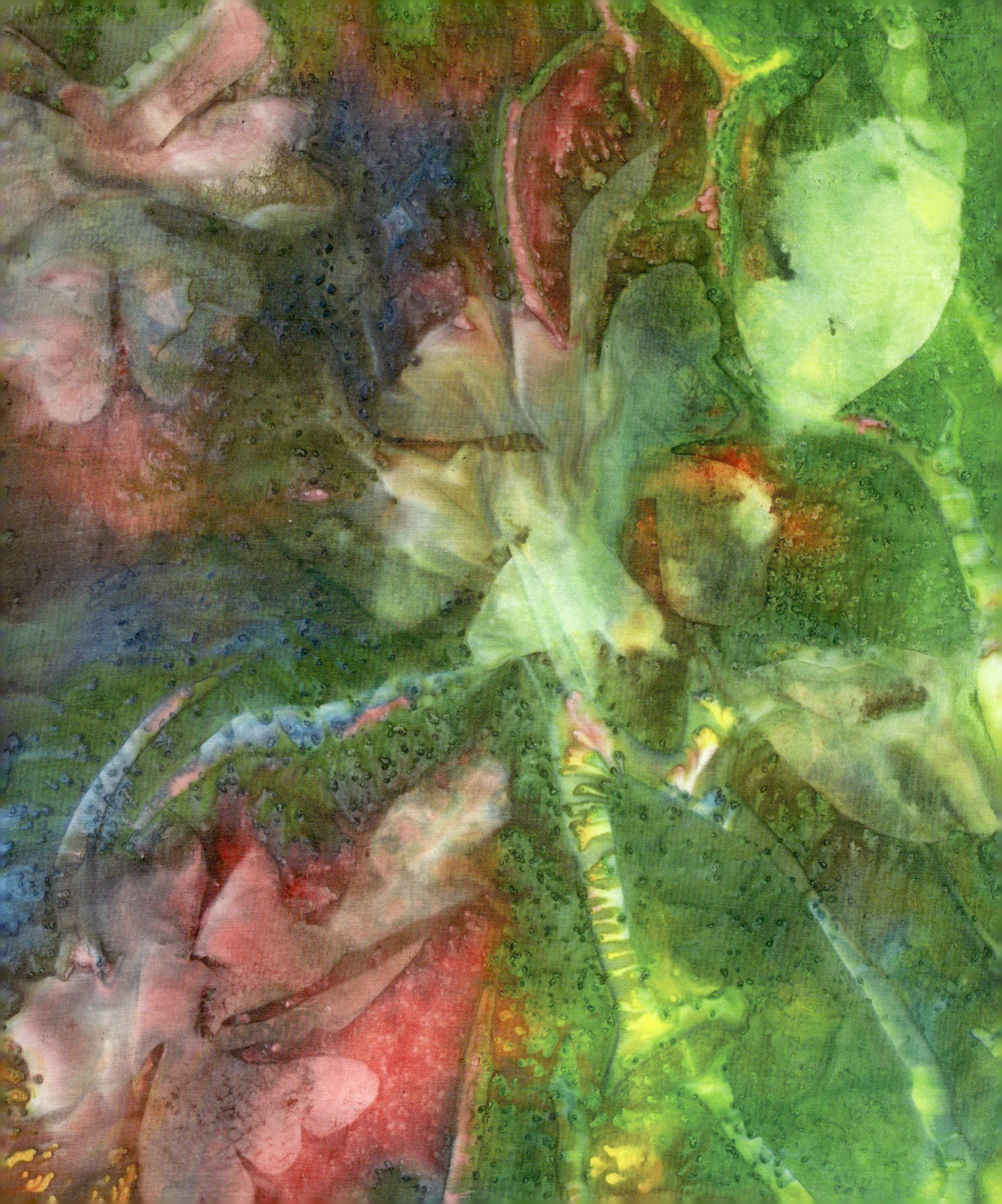

Beagle Bay

In 1909, when my mother, Barbara, was four years old, she was taken with her sister, Bella Lynott, and her cousins, from Ruby Plains Station in the east Kimberley, over to Beagle Bay. These 'stolen generation' children were referred to as 'half-castes', and many were children of station managers or owners. At that time throughout Australia, it was government policy to remove half-caste children from their Aboriginal mothers and place them in missions or government institutions.

My mother never forgot that trip on the back of the horse and sulky from Halls Creek to Wyndham and then by boat from Wyndham to Broome. As children we were told stories of this terrifying trip over and over again. Aunty Bella talked about the first night on the boat when the girls refused to eat. When they were leaving, their mothers had warned them to be careful about the food in case the *gardiya* (white man) tried to poison them. On the first night the children were given sausages for supper. They had never seen such food before, and they quickly threw the sausages overboard, shouting *'Gurra! Gurra!'* They thought it was the white men's faeces.

From Broome, the children were taken on a pearling lugger to Beagle Bay. Aunty Bella got very sick on the trip and had to be carried from the boat to the mission. She was only seven and I think she was overcome by all the changes that had occurred. Unlike some of the younger children, she was old enough to understand what was happening. They were being taken from their families into completely unknown territory. The older children were told to look after the younger ones. They were able to tell them stories of their 'country', and to clarify relationships with each other as best as children could.

Two of my mother's uncles from Halls Creek, Charlie and Paddy, were also on the journey. They were both 'full-bloods' and were being taken to the mission because they had been caught stealing goats. They were about fifteen years old and had much

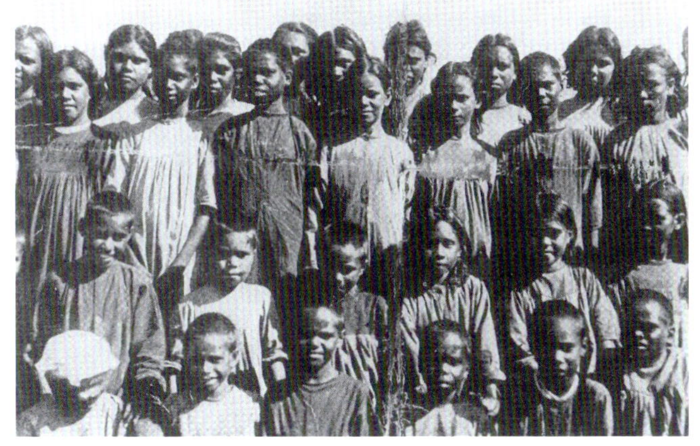

Beagle Bay Mission, c1910s. My mother is in the centre of the third row, next to Aunty Willa (right) and Aunty Bella at the end (far right).

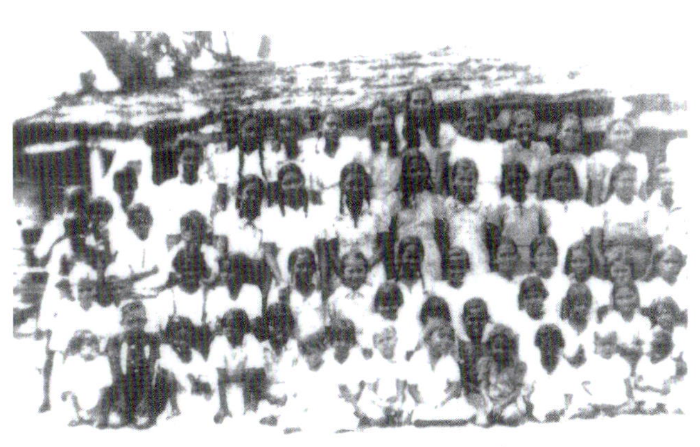

Broome evacuees during the war years, Beagle Bay. I'm told the baldhead baby in the front row is me!

knowledge of the traditions of their homeland. I am sure the others would have lost their identity and heritage if Uncle Charlie and Uncle Paddy had not been around.

Now, many years later, and about to be the mother of three children, my mother found herself once more on an anxious and traumatic journey to Beagle Bay. She hadn't been back to the mission since being sent to the convent in Broome when she was fourteen years old. In those days girls were sent from the mission down to the convent to be groomed and trained as domestics. Many of them ended up working for pearling masters and other European families. My mother worked for Mr Carrick, the manager of the NSW Bank, and she always spoke very highly of him and his wife.

The Nyul Nyul people from Beagle Bay were already settled at the mission, and with the arrival of the Broome evacuees, its population nearly doubled in size. Many of the local people gave up their houses for the newcomers. The group of women and children being evacuated with my mother and sister, Pearl, also had to be housed and fed, and they ended up squatting in one house. This experience brought the families very close together, and there were many mothers and 'aunties' who made the children feel safe during the war years.

It didn't take long to settle into mission life. Mum remembered how beautiful Beagle Bay could be. The plants grew thick and green, fed by the water from underground freshwater springs. Water lilies that were pink, violet, yellow and white floated on pools of water, lined with bulrushes and pandanus. Green lawn ran wild, and it was a tropical garden in the bush during the humid wet season. However, this wasn't always the case because Beagle Bay could also be a cold, damp place in the dry season. Some mornings there would be ice in the taps, and if you left a bucket of water out at night it would turn to ice.

On 24 April, 1942, with the help of the midwives, Aunty Grace Martin (who would become my godmother) and Aunty Alice Wright, my brother Jimmy and I came into the world — I came out second. Mum lost a lot of blood during our birth, and it was Mother Alphonsus who saved my mother's life. She sat on Mum's bed and urged her to suck on liver to replenish her blood.

'Come on Barbara, you can't give up, you've got three children to live for.'

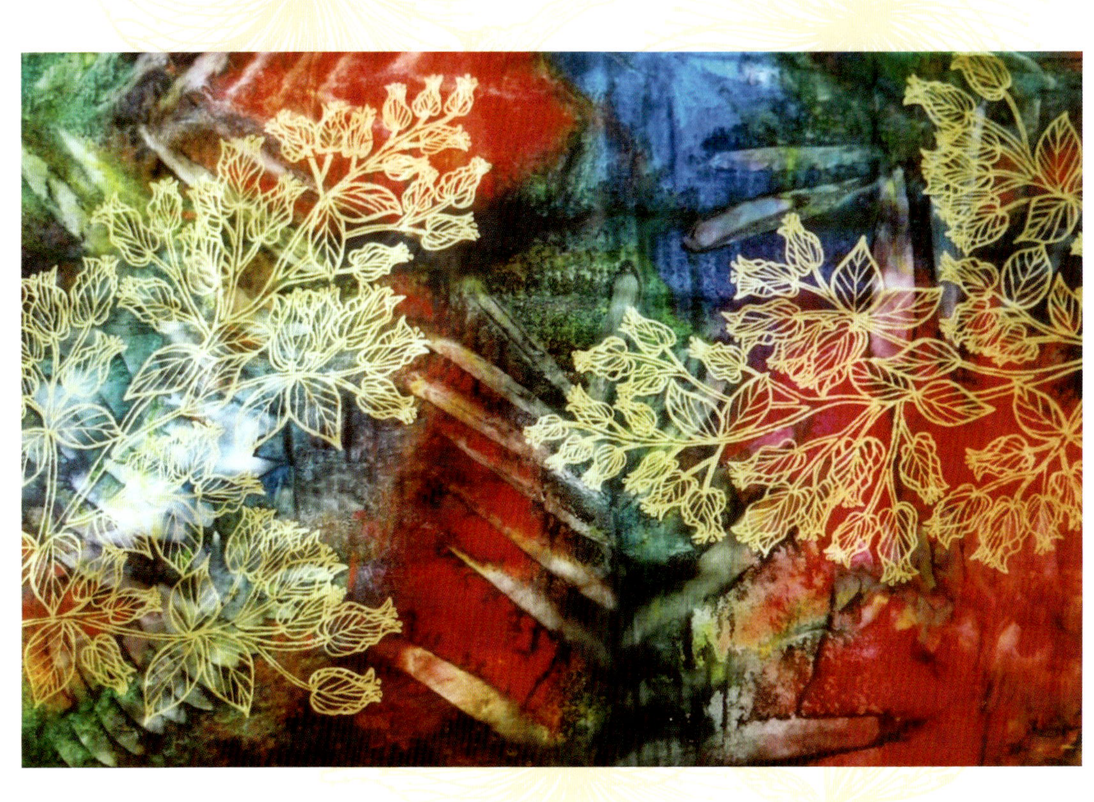

Bougainvillea Gold

Mother Alphonsus nursed at Beagle Bay during the war, and then went out to the leprosarium near Derby. The St John of God nuns were trained nurses as well as being exceptional teachers. They played an important role in the lives of the Catholic families throughout the Kimberley. All the nuns wore full habits — white with thick, black stockings and shoes, and white veils. I don't know how they survived in that heat when there was no air-conditioning.

Mum took many months to recuperate from the birth, and Aunty Rosie Lee looked after me. She had four children of her own, but she took me in and cared for me. Aunty Elsie Taylor, Rosie's sister, cared for Jimmy. Aunty Bella, who lived and worked at the Holy Child Orphanage, looked after Pearl. Throughout my childhood, Aunty Rosie kept an eye on me and, even today, I am still very close to her daughters, Joyce and Mary-Rose.

Jimmy and I were baptised one week after our birth, and my godfather was a Filipino man called Sebastian. Baptisms happened soon after the birth in case the baby didn't survive. I was baptised Ursula Selina Drummond — Ursula after my godmother, Aunty Ursula Grace Martin — but over the years I learnt to answer to Sally. When Jimmy was ten months old, he died from pneumonia. It was accepted and not uncommon that babies could be stillborn or die when young.

Pneumonia was almost a sure death and families were terrified of a child getting sick because there were no doctors at Beagle Bay.

The building of the large, white, Spanish-style, stone church was one of the biggest undertakings at the mission. Everybody at Beagle Bay had a role to play in the building of the Sacred Heart Church, and they went about their work with great pride. My mother, Aunties Bella, Margaret and Willa, and the other girls had to sort the shells that were to be used to decorate the inside of the church, into sizes and colour. The shell sorting was done in the afternoons under the guidance and instruction of the priests and brothers, and it was the pearl shells that were used to form the magnificent altar. The size of this church, for a little girl like me, was awesome and the building is still recognised today as a masterpiece.

The masses and benedictions were said in Latin and the responses were sung back to the priests. The hymns were sung with first and second part harmonies. It was sublime. The choir was beautiful and the smell of incense intoxicating. My mother always talked with affection about the Beagle Bay church. It gave her a sense of ownership, belonging and pride.

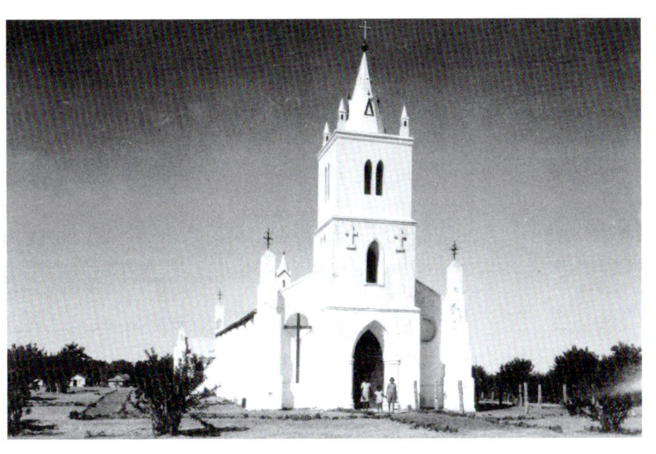

Sacred Heart Church,
Beagle Bay, 1953.

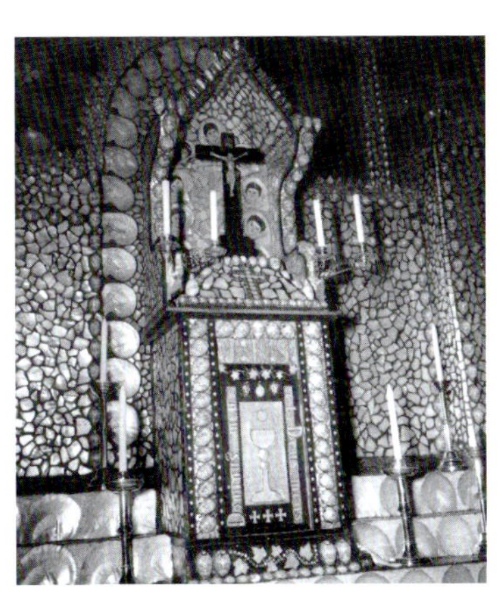

Pearl shell altar,
Sacred Heart Church,
Beagle Bay.

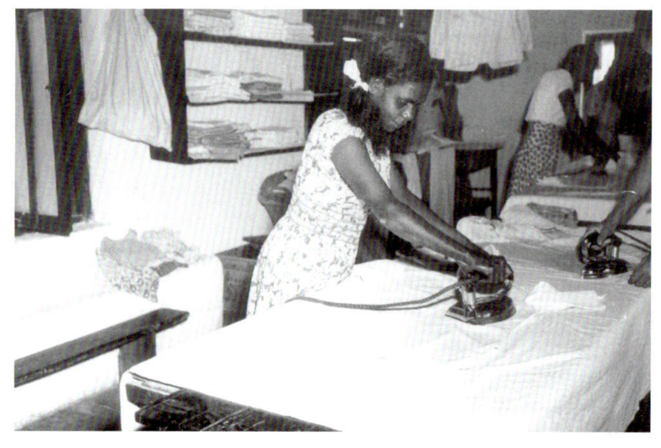

The girls at Beagle Bay were trained in domestic skills, 1953.

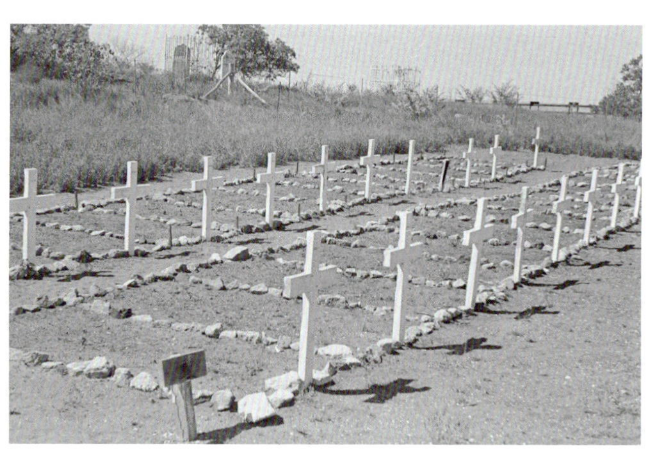

The Dutch war cemetery, Broome, 1948.

Mass was always packed, and I recall being outside and kneeling on the hard gravel for the service. The Aboriginal altar boys were dressed in long, white robes and the priest in full regalia. There were also the Aboriginal sisters from Lombadina and Beagle Bay. They dressed in blue and were known as the 'native sisters'. They helped with the work at the convent and lived a religious life.

During festival celebrations, the church was lit up and people came from everywhere as it was very social. We *always* dressed up to go to church —we *always* put on our Sunday best. If we didn't have good clothes then we made sure the clothes we had on were spotless. Church was a place of reverence and respect. The church was kept very clean and tidy, as was the entire mission.

My mother used to say that even though life was not easy, it was simple. People did not have much and they had to endure long days of hard work. Because the women and girls were trained in domestic skills, they were excellent cooks, housekeepers and dressmakers. Their sewing and crochet work was exquisite. The men were trained in trades such as welding, carpentry and mechanics, and worked as butchers and bakers. Some of the men worked with Brother Sacks, and they grew the vegetables and produced the dairy products.

Many of the people at Beagle Bay had not only been dispossessed from their country, but they had to carry the pain of being separated from their families. There were also constant reminders of the war. Planes would fly low to the ground over the mission, and everyone would run to the bush and hide. The Japanese were chasing the planes that were carrying Dutch refugees escaping from Indonesia.

I was three when we returned to Broome. It was 4 December, 1945. We travelled all night and I lay huddled on the back of the truck, covered by an old, grey army blanket that was wet and smelt like pee.

Back in Broome, the park near the jetty (now known as Old Jetty), next to 'Bathing Shed Beach' (now known as Town Beach), was full of white crosses for all the Dutch nationals who had died during the Japanese bombing of Roebuck Bay in March, 1942. The Dutch had been evacuated from Java and had been moored in the bay in flying boats. There were a few survivors but over forty people lost their lives. Years later some of their families came and took their remains back to Holland. The airplane wrecks lay in a deep lugger channel and were clearly visible at low tide. On very low tides there was a small amount of time when you could get across the channel to go fishing or exploring off the wrecks. When I was older, I would watch the boys go out but I didn't have the courage to follow. It was too frightening watching them swim back when the tide had turned.

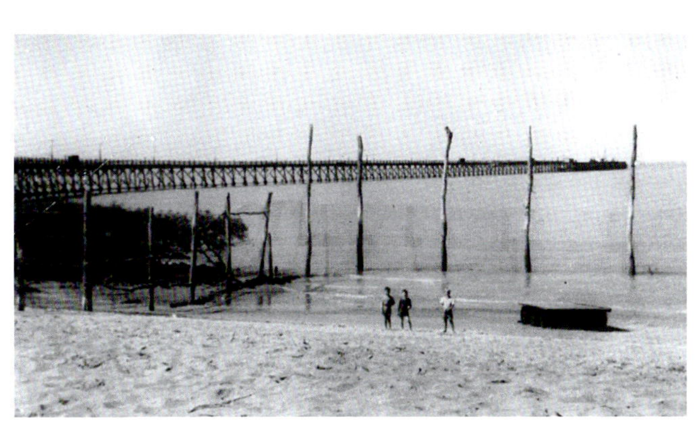

Low tide at Bathing Shed Beach, 1950s.

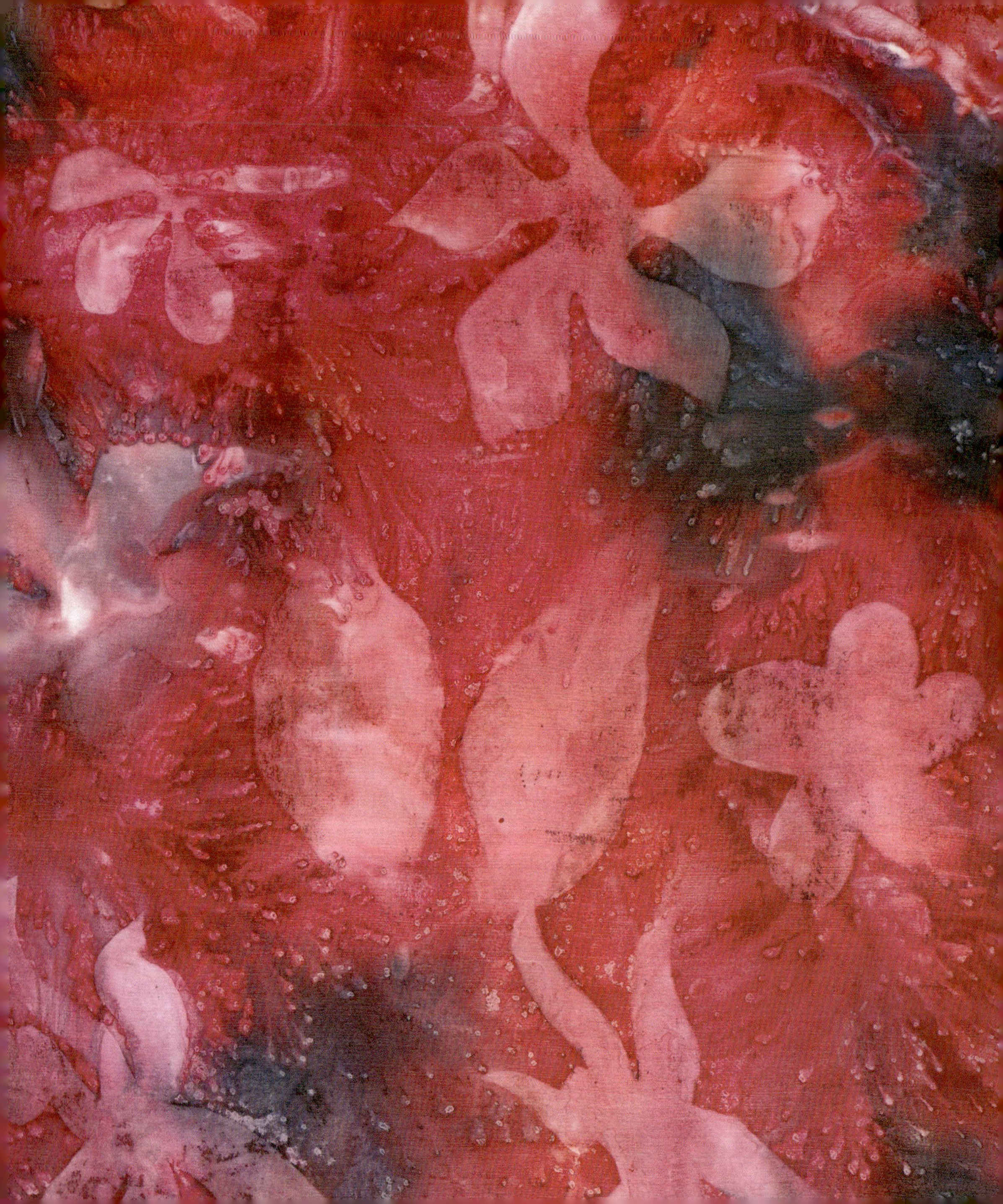

Holy Child Orphanage

The war had a big impact on Broome because everybody was removed. In 1942 all the women, European and Asian, and their children were evacuated south. Most of the coloureds and full-bloods went to Beagle Bay. Those Japanese that had married women of Aboriginal descent were interned with their families. My mother's cousin, Margaret Shiosaki, was interned with her husband and children in Melbourne. I remember my mother worrying about their safety and she would ask us to pray for them. It was only after the war that we heard they had returned to Western Australia and settled down near Geraldton.

After the war, the population was scattered. No-one knew what the future held as there were few jobs, and many children were separated from their parents. These children were eventually taken to a cluster of buildings in Barker Street — the Holy Child Orphanage, run by the St John of God nuns.

The police would often deliver girls to the orphanage on behalf of the Native Welfare Department. Many of the girls were stolen generation kids, mainly from the East Kimberley, as well as girls who had Asian fathers in Broome. There was Fay and Georgina Kassim, Julie and Pauline Mamid, and Betty Hassan, and we all bonded together. Pearl and I stayed at the orphanage until Mum got a job at the Broome District Hospital as a ward maid and found somewhere for us to live.

There was a dormitory for the older girls and one for the younger girls. There were no boys at the orphanage, they were sent to Beagle Bay. The boys' nickname for the orphanage girls was the 'blue army' because the nuns used to walk them to school, two by two, like soldiers in their blue uniforms.

Because Aunty Bella worked there, Pearl and I often spent our weekends or days of the school holidays at the orphanage when mum was at work. There were bullies and cliques among the girls, but the bigger girls would look after me, especially Lena Smith.

The orphanage received charity clothing boxes from all over

Australia, full of cardigans, dresses and blouses. If something fitted, you could take your pick. We all wore sandals to school and church, but my very best shoes were shiny black, patent leather. My hair was kept short because of my curls, but the other girls tied their long, straight hair back with a ribbon, or wore it in a bun or plaits.

The best times were the camping trips out to one of the many beaches around Broome. We'd travel out to our camping spots on one of Mr Pryor's trucks. Mr Pryor was a wood cutter and he had a fleet of trucks. Wood was one of the main fuels as there was no gas or electricity, and every house needed wood for cooking. Mr Pryor would have people chopping wood, and the trucks would collect it and deliver it to customers' homes. The trucks were numbered 1, 2, 3 and 4, and the nuns would hire them for school picnics and the races. Everybody would yell, 'Inter coming!' and the grey truck with its long, wooden tray would pull up. A lot of excited girls would scramble onto the back, and the driver would go to the front of the truck and crank the engine. Off we'd roar, over the red, corrugated dirt, through piles of soft sand, laughing and singing at the tops of our voices.

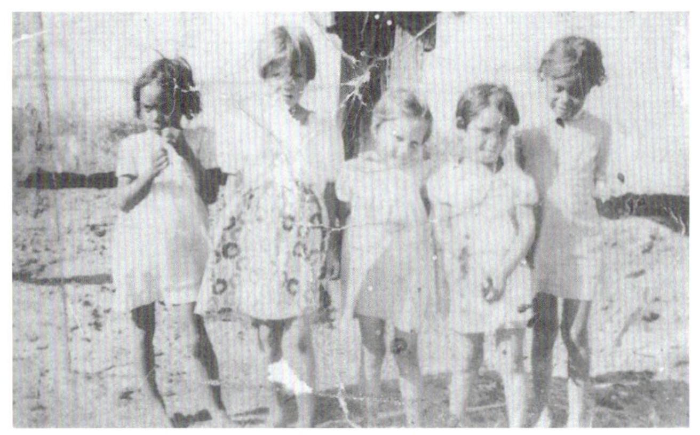

Under the jetty with the orphanage girls —
Betty Hassan, Shirley Thompson, Patsy Downs,
Marjorie Angela and myself, c1948.

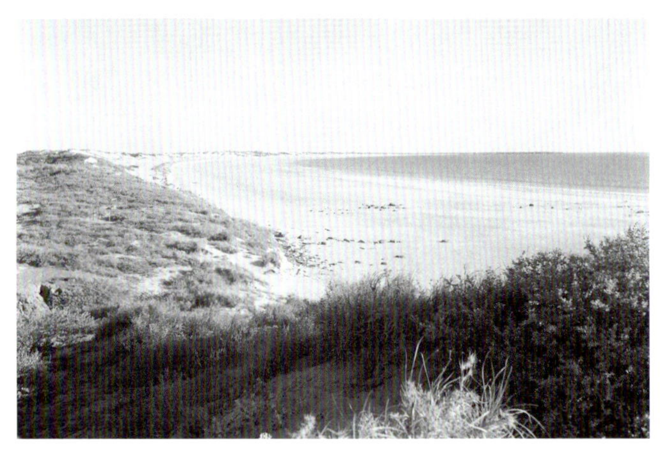

Cable Beach, 1953.

Sometimes we would head out to the white stretch of coast known as Cable Beach — it got its name from the communication cable that ran from Broome to Java in Indonesia. We would make a day camp just below the cliff edge that gently fell away down to the beach, and take a big canvas sheet and hang it from long poles for shade. We usually had the whole fourteen miles of pristine, white sand and glistening, turquoise water to ourselves.

Cable Beach was often covered with shells — cowries, olives, broken pearl shells, scallops, cockles, starfish, turbans and spider shells. We loved collecting them off the beach, or off the reefs. When the tide was out, we'd be on the reefs searching for cowries and corals to paint, or tiger and money cowries to trade with each other.

During the turtle season the tracks of the females would mark the beach. At night the females would lay their eggs, and if you got there early in the morning, you would see them making their way back to the water.

When we camped at Lighthouse Beach, now known as Gantheaume Point, we had Mr Percy's old house to stay in. We'd camp on the verandahs with no mattresses, only blankets. Years before Anastasia Percy had lived at the lighthouse with her husband.

She was disabled with arthritis and Mr Percy had built a little concrete pool down amongst the rocks at Gantheaume Point, so that she could bathe when the tide filled it. We called it 'Percy Pool', but more recently it has become known as 'Anastasia's Pool'.

When I was about four, I was out with the orphanage girls swimming in Percy Pool and we were all jumping and splashing around. Suddenly I began screaming my head off and all the girls looked frantically to see what was wrong. It was discovered that I had a little turtle hanging off my ear!

Out at the lighthouse there were bushes with long yellow flowers which we called 'emu flowers'. There were always emus out at the lighthouse — they also used to come into the marsh around town when the tide was out. We'd be walking across the marsh with our bread and milk and the emus would chase us.

Eventually the big house at the lighthouse got pulled down, and when it was no longer there we stayed in the guesthouse, a little cottage next door. I can still recall that it had absolutely no furniture. After that we would have our school picnics over at Fatima, the nuns' house on Crab Creek Road.

When the nuns had their beach house at Redell Beach, we went there every Christmas holidays. We would camp for a week with Aunty Bella and the orphanage girls, and would spend our days fishing, swimming and exploring the reef. We used to wear rompers, a bit like jumpsuits with little bib-style fronts. We wore those rompers for years, and I remember checking out the other girls' chests to see how things were developing. Sometimes we'd jump into the water with everything on — shorts and shirts, or bathers, with the shirred elastic stretch-top. We thought we were great.

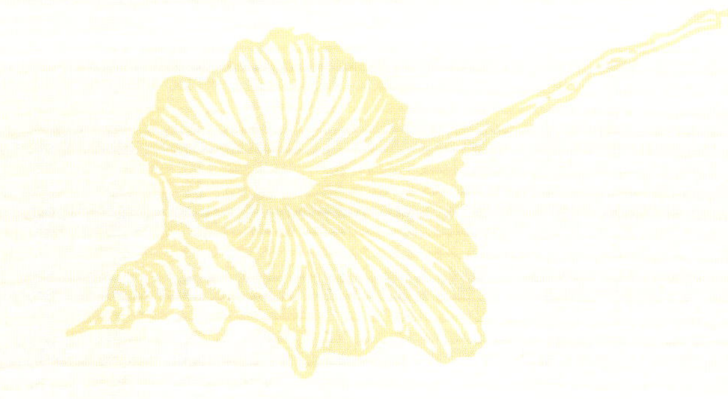

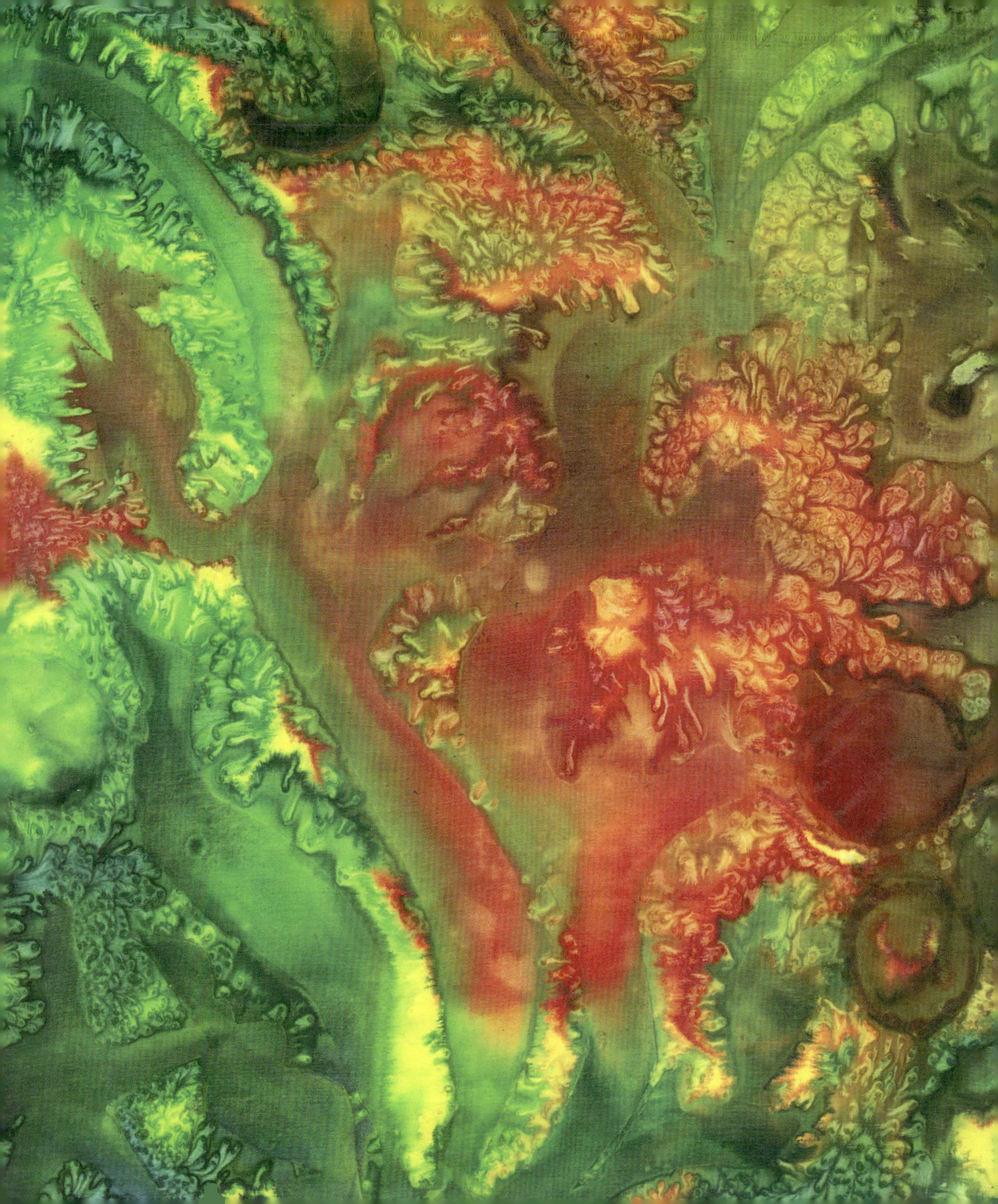

Multiculturalism

When people come to Broome, they are sometimes surprised by the way people look, and they do not expect the Aboriginal and Asian mix. The pearling industry, however, had attracted people from Asian countries and beyond since the 1880s, and it is their descendents that make up the multicultural population of the town today.

We also had religious orders working in Broome and the Kimberley from European countries such as Germany, Ireland and Spain. As children we didn't know that the rest of Australia was not like Broome, and we took for granted the many ethnic groups who lived together. We had the world at our doorstep.

In the homes I grew up in, Malay and English were the common languages, and children with Malay fathers learnt to speak a Broome-style Malay at home. This form of Malay had a lot of Indonesian mixed in. It was the easiest language to learn and was spoken on the luggers by everyone, including the Aboriginal people and the Europeans.

Aboriginal languages such as Bardi, Nyul Nyul, Yawuru, Jaru and Karijarri were also spoken. Aunties would come to our house for gambling and play card games, like kuncan and poker, and we would sit and listen to their stories. They spoke in languages from all over the Kimberley, not just the Broome area — places like Lombadina, Beagle Bay, Halls Creek. Before my mother was taken away as a child, she spoke Jaru from the East Kimberley, and we picked up a few words. She also knew some Yawuru and would occasionally speak it to us.

Mum's mother-in-law, *Mimi* (Granny) Polly was a Yawuru woman. When Mum's husband was taken to the leprosarium near Derby, Mum lived with her and Mimi Polly taught her some Yawuru language. If she was annoyed with me she would yell, *'Bagu ngandira, wirrib nganyju juyu, wirdugun balu!'* This roughly translates as, 'Come here, girl, or I might hit you with this big stick!' I think I

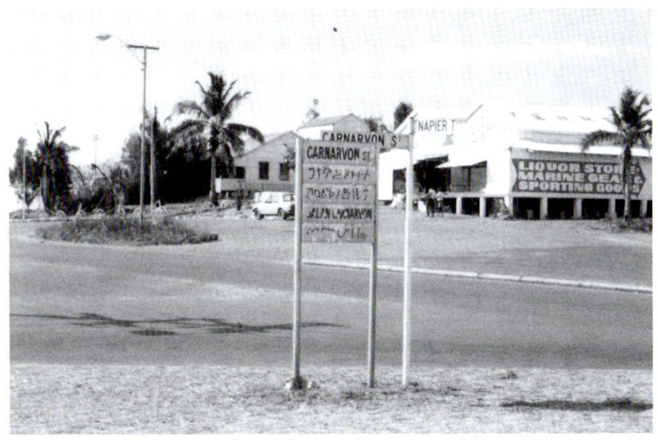

Chinatown, 1960s.

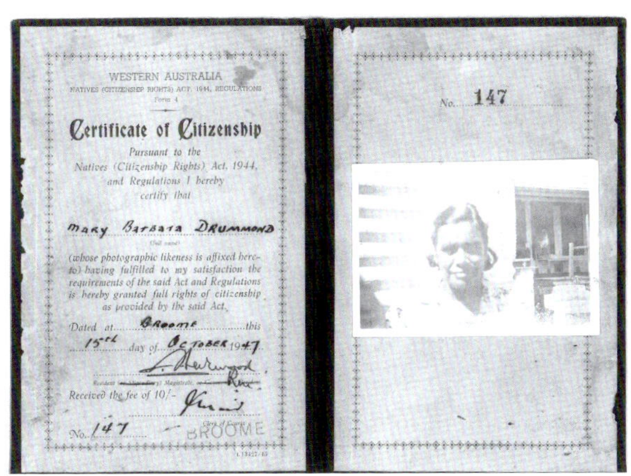

WESTERN AUSTRALIA

NATIVES (CITIZENSHIP RIGHTS) ACT, 1944, REGULATIONS

Form 4

Certificate of Citizenship

Pursuant to the Natives (Citizenship Rights) Act, 1944, and Regulations I hereby certify that

Mary Barbara Drummond
(full name)

(whose photographic likeness is affixed hereto) having fulfilled to my satisfaction the requirements of the said Act and Regulations is hereby granted full rights of citizenship as provided by the said Act.

Dated at Broome *this* 15th *day of* October 1947

Resident Magistrate

Received the fee of 10/-

Clerk of Courts

No. 147 BROOME

No. 147

My mother's
'Certificate of Citizenship'.

must have been a ratbag. It's the only Yawuru sentence I can speak.

Of course there were many other languages heard in the town, including those spoken by the Chinese, Malay, Japanese, Ceylonese, Indonesian, and Filipino workers. Consequently the town had a great mix of religions, and there were Buddhists, Muslims, Shintoists, Christians, Hindus and Jews. We generally respected and accepted each other's religion and culture, and it was really only the Europeans who tried to change us. They wanted everyone to be more like them, and in some ways they would exclude people that were different. Any name they couldn't pronounce was Europeanised.

People were classified into racial groups and given status accordingly. There were the whites or Europeans, the coloureds who were the mixed races, the half-castes who were Aboriginal and European, and the quarter-castes, octoroons and full-bloods. We didn't think much of these labels, but these terms were used by the authorities to determine where you could go and what you could do. Half-caste and mixed-race children could be taken away from their parents to be grown up in an orphanage or on a mission.

Full-blood Aboriginal people could only come into Broome through the 'common gate' if they had a permit. The common gate was a fence that ran through Broome and prevented Aboriginal people from moving freely or living in the town. In the 1940s the State Government decided to allow some Aboriginal people the right to apply for citizenship. This meant they had to live a European lifestyle and they were granted certain privileges, like being able to go into a hotel and buy alcohol. If Europeans gave alcohol to half-castes or full-bloods that didn't have citizenship papers, they could be gaoled.

Some people thought that it was wise to hide your heritage in order to get work or be accepted. We were all classified by our degree of Aboriginality, the more you had, the less you were accepted. Now there is a good feeling about claiming your Aboriginal heritage, but then it was something society made you feel deeply ashamed of.

Even for the women, there was a social hierarchy in the town. If your husband was a diver, rather than a shell cleaner or general crew, you had a higher status. If he was head diver and in charge of all the luggers in that company, then his position held more prestige. These layers of status flowed over into everyone's lives.

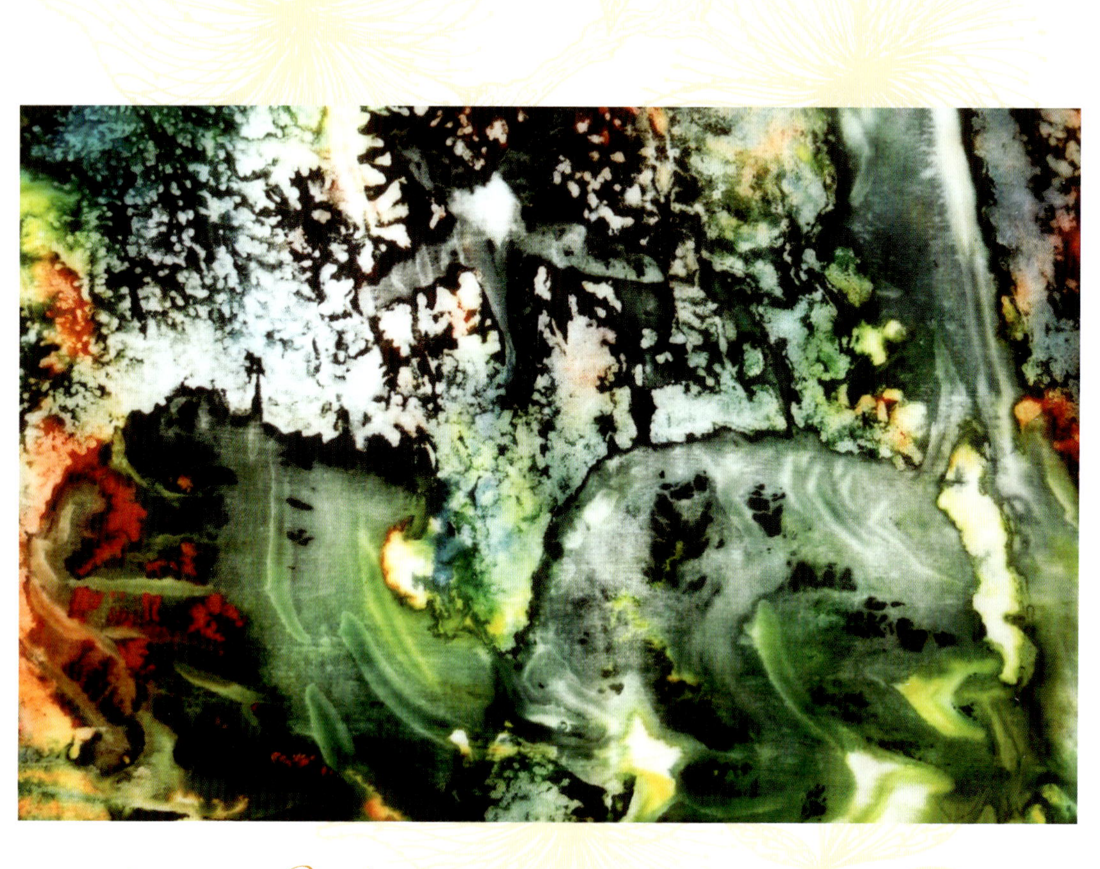

Bubbling Reef

Nowadays it is hard to imagine that Broome was such a multicultural town. Asian families owned many of the businesses and shops, and in the afternoons you would see old Chinamen resting on their verandahs in deck chairs and smoking their pipes.

People were clear about where they came from, and identity was linked to the place you were born. There were that many Ahmats, a common Malay name, much like John in English. So that we knew who we were talking about, some men had names like 'Ahmat Gold-Teeth' and 'Ahmat Cowboy'. Many used the name of the place they came from, like 'Ahmat Jawa', 'Ahmat Saigon' and 'Ahmat Siam'. There was also 'Ahmat Chantik', so-called because of his good looks.

Other aspects of Broome life reflected the town's cultural mix, and it was a common sight to see men on the foreshore in the cool of the morning, or as the sun was going down, doing the slow, precise movements of *tai chi*, or the martial art known as *silat* from Malaysia. A game similar to volleyball called *sepak raga* was brought from Singapore and Malaysia, and the men played it on the foreshore. They would kick a cane ball over a net rather than use their hands.

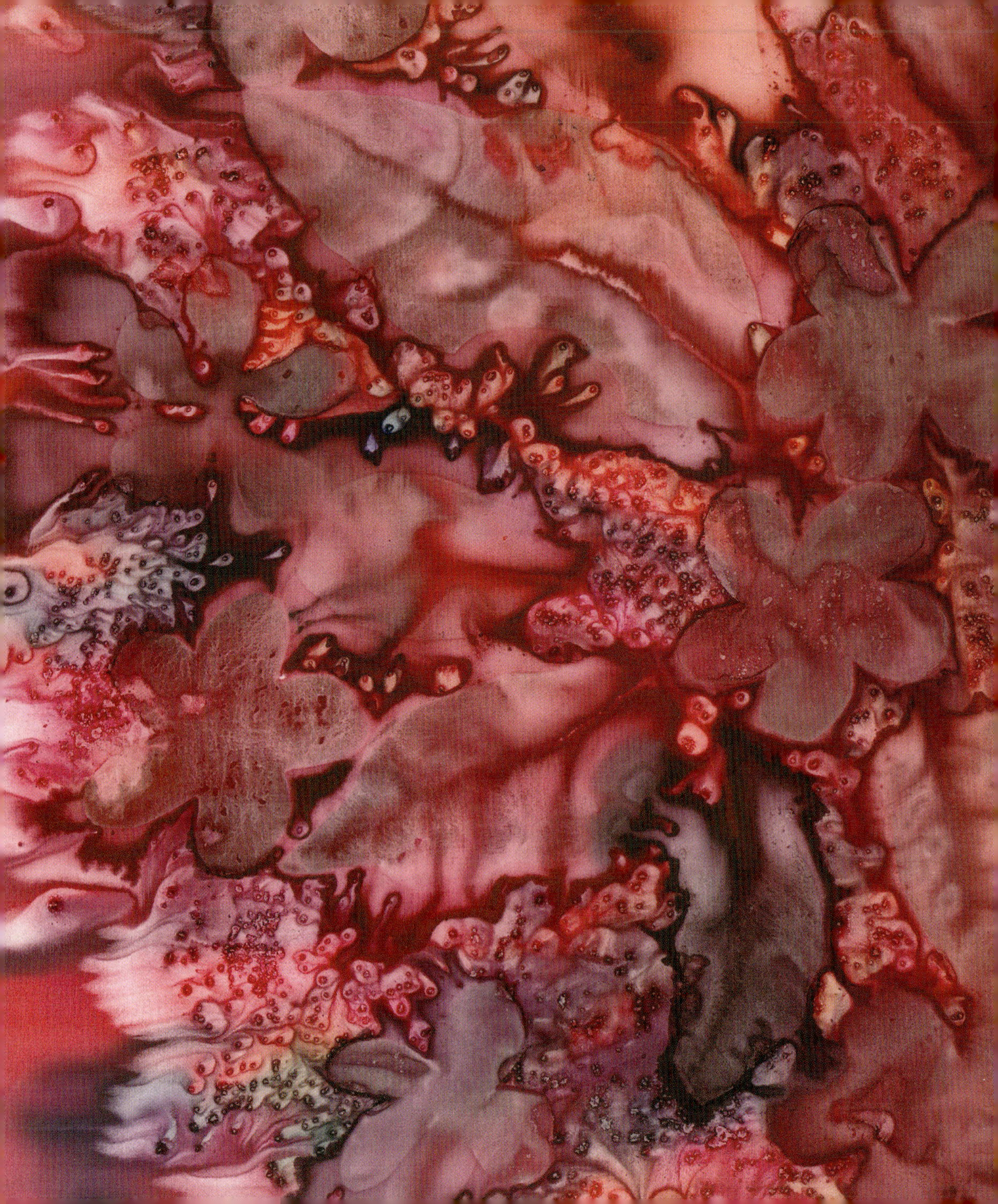

Simeon

My mother met Simeon Bin Said, a Malay from Singapore, and they decided to settle down together. We were to be a family for the next fifty years, although Mum was unable to marry Simeon because she was still married to Cass Drummond. Uncle Cass had been sent away to the leprosarium in Derby not long after they were married. He spent the next thirty years there. Once you were admitted to the leprosarium it was like a life sentence. Some people were cured in two years or five, but many stayed for the rest of their lives. People were not allowed to visit and it was very difficult for those that were separated from their families.

Many women in Broome, and throughout the Kimberley, were left on their own and were forced to bring up their children

hand-pumped the luggers all the way back to Broome. He eventually graduated to deep-sea diver and ended up working on the luggers for many years. Simeon never returned to Singapore and remained in Broome for the rest of his life.

During the war, some of the Malays and Indonesians who had been living in Broome worked as interpreters in the Australian Special Forces. Simeon was sent to New Guinea, and apart from the celebrated local 'Fuzzy Wuzzy Angels' who helped the Australian servicemen on the Kokoda Track, he was the only other coloured man fighting with the army at Bougainville.

After the war, a lot of the Malay and Indonesian men returned to Broome. Some of those enlisted were discharged in Melbourne and found their way home with European wives and families. They started working on the luggers again, but years later when the Japanese were allowed to return as pearl divers, they were replaced and left unemployed. Without Australian citizenship and with no jobs, the men were not able to stay in Australia. Simeon was threatened with deportation even though he had served Australia during the war. Fortunately, he was offered a job in Onslow with

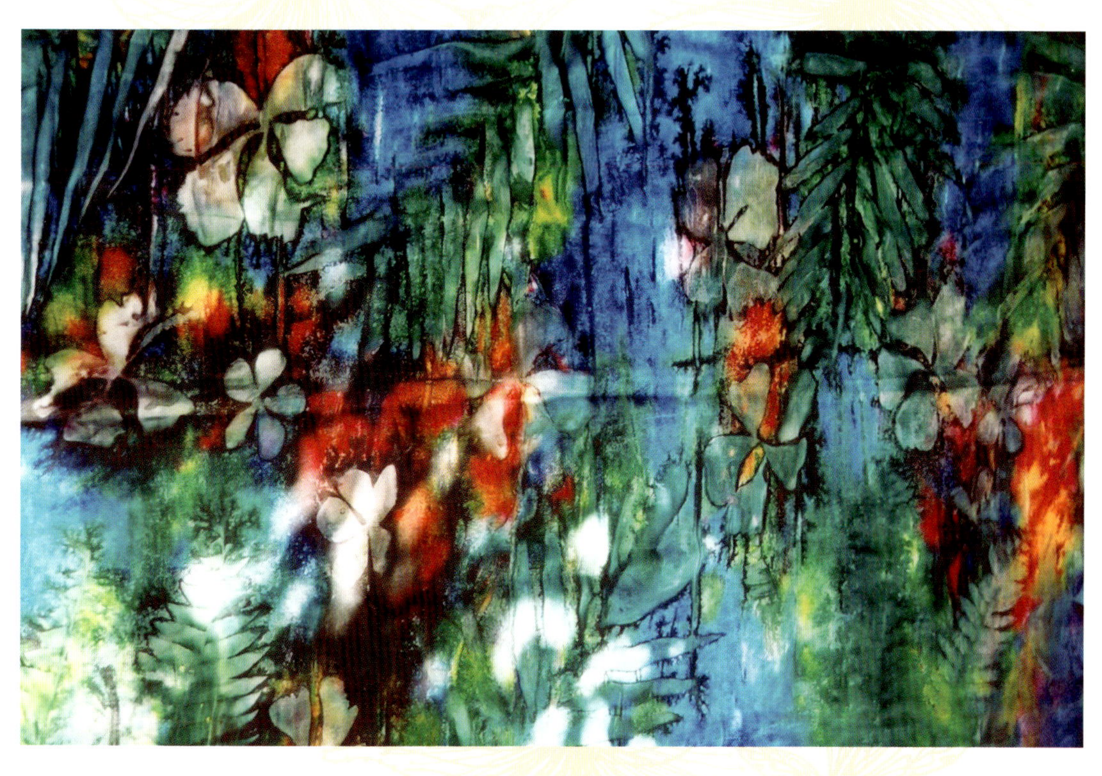

Evening Bloom

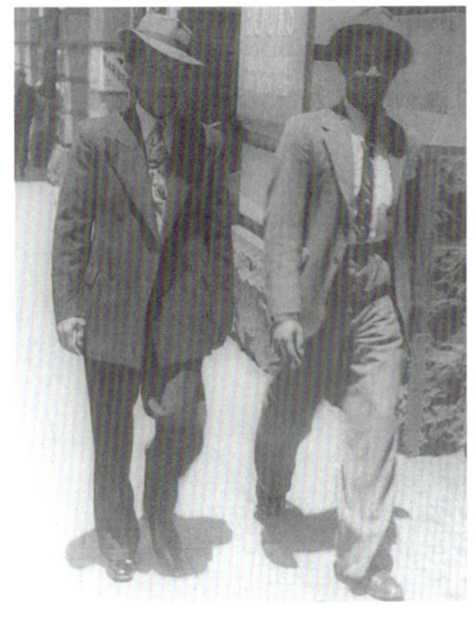

Simeon (left) in Perth after he had been discharged.

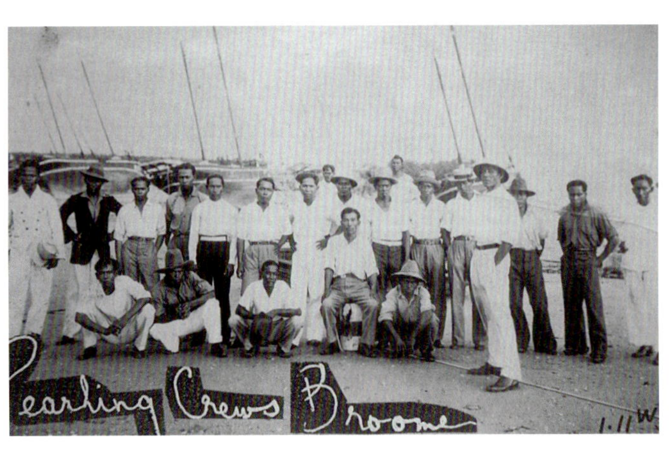

Malay and Indonesian lugger crew after the war. Uncle Salem Bin Sallik is on the far right.

the Clark Pearling Company and he went there, returning to us during the lay-up at Christmas time.

Many of the displaced men eventually took their families and moved to Darwin to secure pearling work. The Returned Services League (RSL) in Darwin supported these ex-servicemen, assisting the men to get 'free papers' or Australian citizenship. They also helped with rehousing and education.

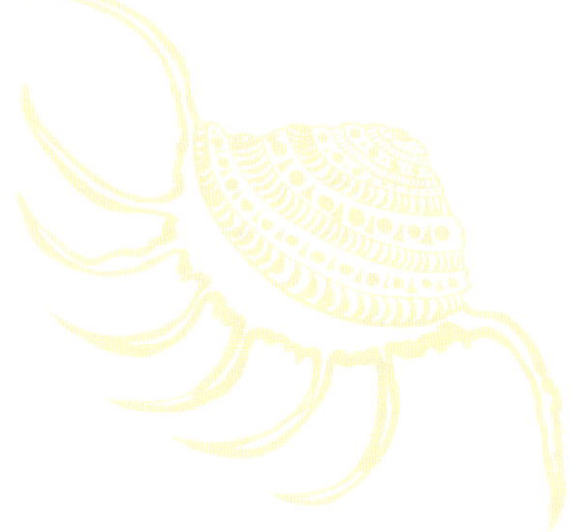

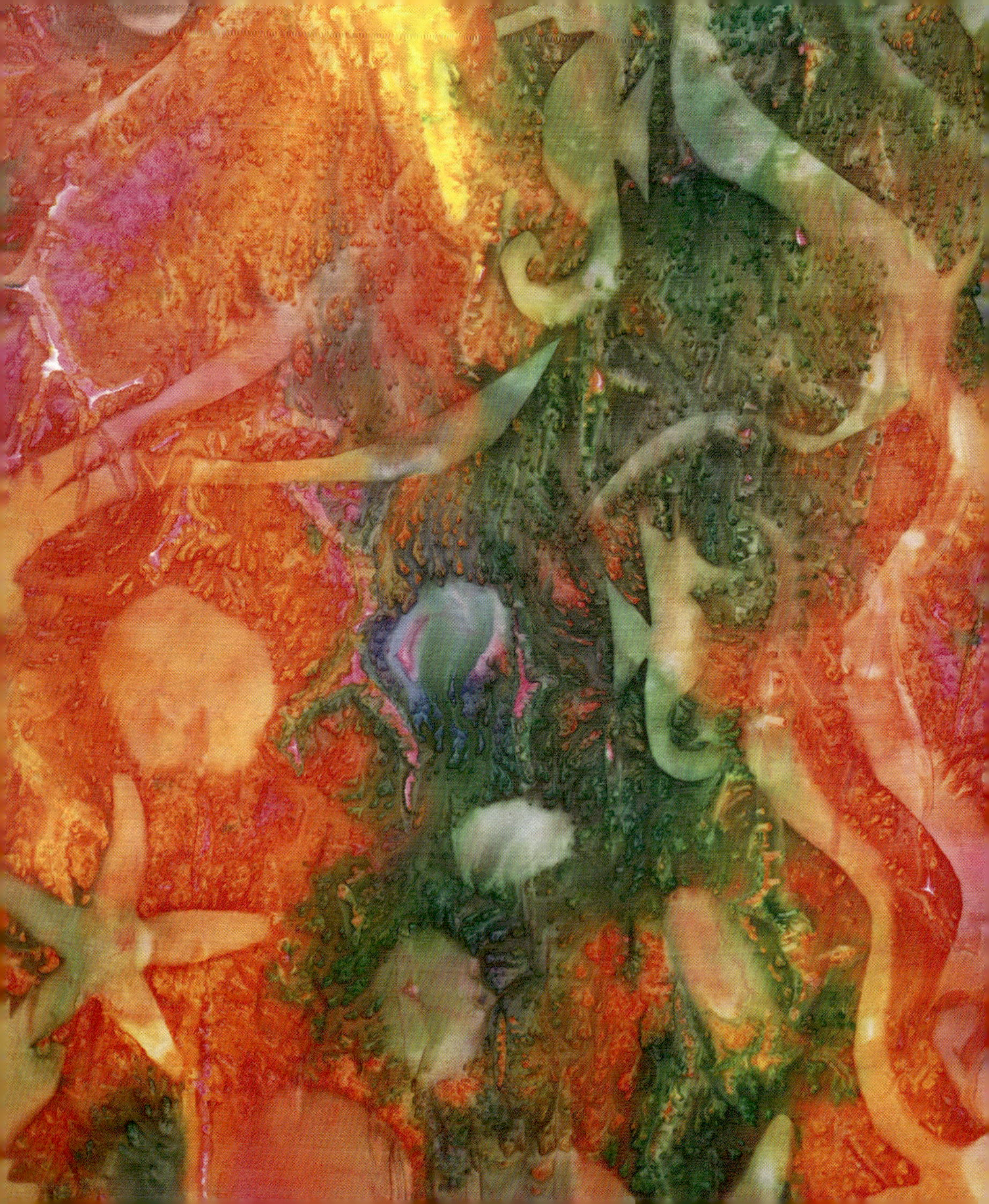

The Long House

One of the first houses we lived in after we left the orphanage was on Robinson Street. It was built, like many Broome houses, out of corrugated iron and large shutters, instead of windows, to let in the breeze. I called it the 'Long House' because of its shape. I was about four when we moved into the Long House.

We lived in the Long House with four other families, and it was communal living. There were Christians, Muslims, Buddhists and one Hindu all sharing one house. The people around us were strong in their faith, and although we had different prayer nights, we all celebrated each other's religious feasts. Simeon was Muslim and my mother was Catholic. She instilled her beliefs in Pearl and myself, and going to a Catholic school helped to strengthen my belief in God. We were encouraged to treat 'others' as we would like them to treat us. We had strict discipline at home and at school, and we were taught that God and religion always came first.

The house was divided into four sections with a communal dining room and separate bedrooms. My family had the front verandah enclosed with lattice because there were only four of us. There was a special prayer room for Con Gill, the Hindu landlord, to pray and make offerings. This prayer room was locked except for two nights each week when Con would go in and pray. It was his sacred space.

Con Gill was a very interesting man. He was from the West Indies — West Indians were among the first people to work in the pearling industry, and Con was the last to remain in Broome. Although he was from the Caribbean, he didn't look all that different to us. Con was tall and slim with kinked hair — black once upon a time, but going grey. He used to wear a green or blue drill shirt and pants, and a gold hoop earring. Like a lot of men, in the winter he wore grey flannel diver's pants. We were very aware of him as he would shuffle along with a cockatoo on his shoulder, humming strange songs.

'Who's this?' we'd say to each other.

'Have a guess who I am?'

'Con Gill!' imitating everything he did and screaming with laughter.

'Don't make fun of him,' our parents used to say. 'That old man got *puri puri* (voodoo).'

I was a teenager when he died. He had no countrymen left.

The head of the household, Ahmat Mustafa, who we called 'Ahmat Jawa' because he was from Java, and his wife, Esther, were in the master bedroom. Aunty Esther was a Filipino–Aboriginal woman. She was the local midwife, and she'd get on her bike and go off to deliver babies at all hours. Mimi Corpus, Esther's mother, was a Yawuru woman and came to our house every night to have a meal. We loved her stories, especially when she used to tell us about her childhood in Broome in the late 1800s. Sitting on Bathing Shed Beach with her mother, she had seen the jetty being built. She lived across the road from the Long House.

Ahmat Jawa had a brother called Pieman, and he came back from Melbourne with his European wife, Betty. They slept behind a curtained area off the kitchen. The Matsumoto family also lived in the house when they returned after the war. Their daughter, Tomako (Eileen), became like a big sister to us.

In the Long House there was beautiful old furniture. Javanese teak cupboards and huge day beds — we took it all for granted. Lots of furniture came off the Blue Funnel Line boats from Singapore — the *Charon*, *Gorgon* and the *Centaur*. I loved the cane furniture and those four-poster beds with canopies. Dutch pillows, now known as bolsters, were brought over by the Indonesians and used on our beds.

We had a small safe made from timber and flywire that we called the kitchenette. It had doors to protect the food from ants, flies and cockroaches. To eat we sat at a big table with long benches down each side. The adults would also use it as a gambling table, with at least twenty people sitting comfortably. At teatime it was quite formal and we never ate without a tablecloth.

A large tamarind tree grew in the yard and there was a date palm in the corner. In the evenings we sat and heard the stories of everyone who lived in the house. If they didn't want us to understand, they would switch to another language. We heard

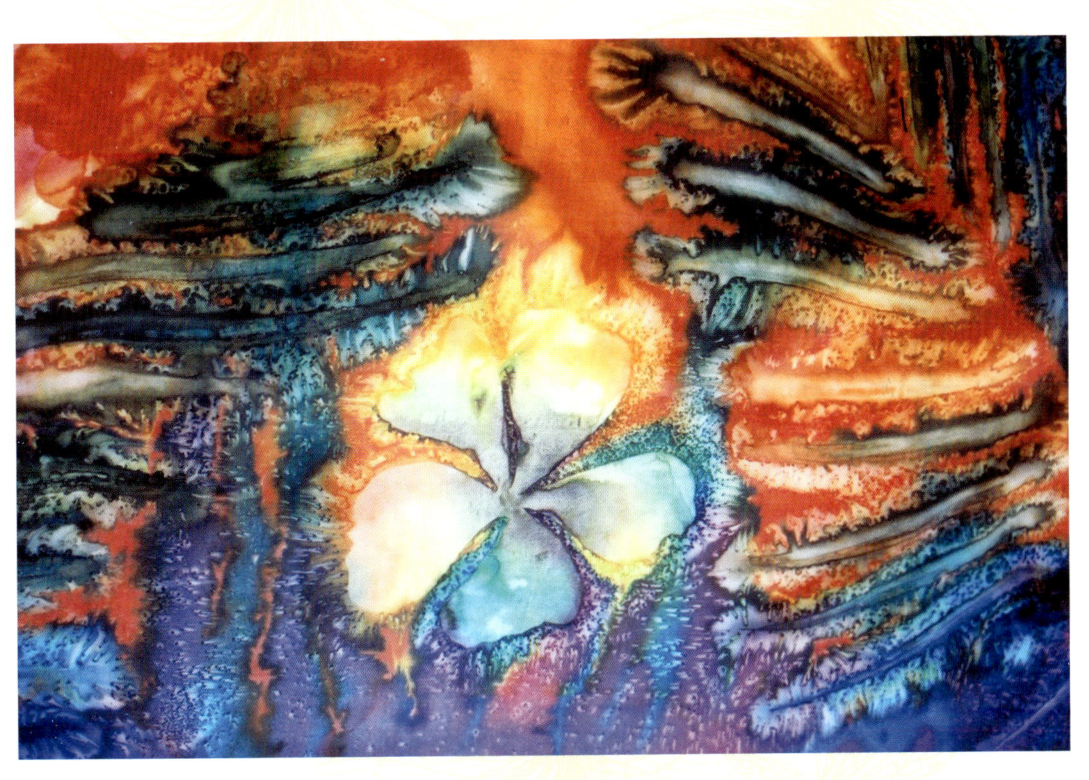

Hibiscus Sunset

stories from all over Asia. Simeon was a great storyteller, and thirty years later when I went to Singapore I felt as if I had been there before. Apart from Con Gill, everyone in the house reminisced about their homelands. We would hear him humming his songs, but that was about all. He was a very private person and although he would always acknowledge us, he never sat and joined in the conversation.

When it was bath time we were told, *'Mandi dulu'*. To bathe we'd use a big enamel dipper in the bath, soaping ourselves and splashing the water over. Some days someone would come right up to the open bathroom and you'd yell, 'Hey, I'm in here!' Luckily there was a latch on the door. I wasn't afraid of frogs or I would never have had a bath — they lined up around the forty-four-gallon drums with their eyes staring from their fat, green bodies, making an incredible noise. The lavatory was down the backyard and at bedtime Mum used to say, 'You go *goomboo* (toilet) before you go to sleep.' We hated going down there in the dark.

Our mother used coal and kettle irons, or flat irons, that were heated on the wood stove. Washing was done by hand using 'Velvet Soap'. Sheets, tablecloths, and clothes were soaked in 'Recketts Blue' to make them whiter. Each house had a copper and when the water was boiled, the clothes were pushed with a heavy stick into the water to kill any germs. Tablecloths, pillowcases and shirts were starched before our mother carefully ironed them.

The Long House had rainwater tanks. People usually had one at each corner of their house to collect the rain. Each tank had a tap and you would go out to the tank to get water for the house. If there were good rains we'd put buckets outside and save the fresh water. The water in the tanks had to last from one rainy season to the next, so everybody was very careful.

The town supply of water that came from an artesian bore near Mary Street was the dirtiest, reddest water I have ever seen. It ran down past the Magistrate's house into the mangroves and Roebuck Bay. The water was so awful you could set your hair without gel. It was mainly used for bathing and the garden, but if our rainwater supply ran out, we had to filter the bore water in clay soya sauce urns filled with gravel. These soya sauce urns came from Singapore for the pearling crews who would bottle the sauce and then give the urns away.

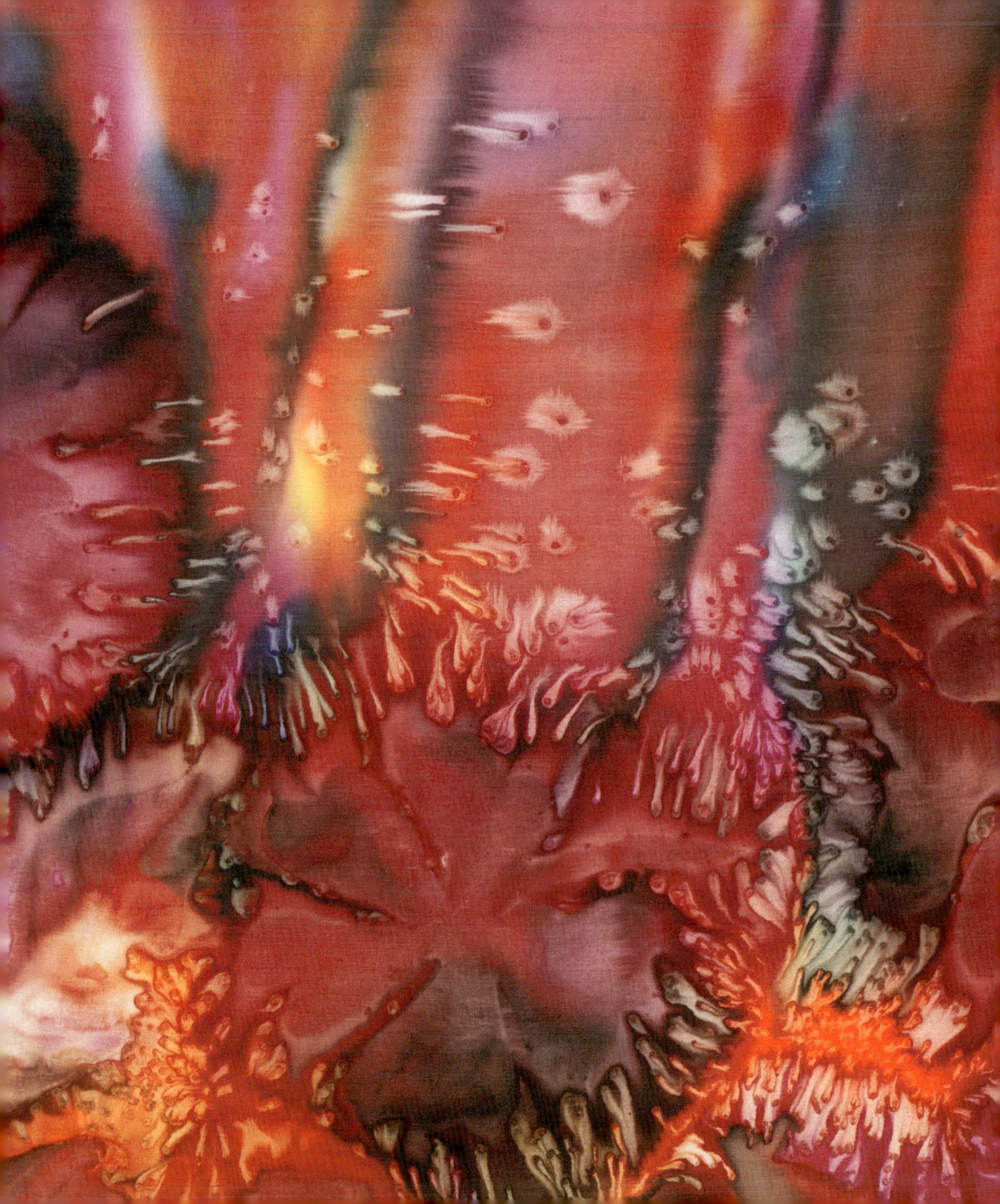

Food

Like most houses in Broome, we had our own veggie garden. We grew everything — beans, tomatoes, sweet potato, Chinese cabbage (bok choy), as well as tropical fruits. Many of the tropical fruits were first introduced to Broome by the Asian crews off the boats from the Blue Funnel Line. The crews were famous for their black market goods, and did a roaring trade selling watches, jewellery and perfume to the coloured people.

They also brought custard apples, bananas, coconuts, paw paws, mangoes and guavas which we began to grow. In the old days, they'd sell them off the train that ran from Chinatown to the jetty. After the war, the train no longer operated and we would go down to the jetty with Simeon and eat fruits like mangosteen and rambutan on the boat. Quarantine regulations meant fruit was not allowed to come on shore.

Other seasonal fruit and vegetables like apples, oranges, and stone fruits, and cabbage and celery came up from Perth. MacRobertson Miller Airlines (MMA) had DC3 planes, which flew twice a week, and the State Ships came fortnightly. By the time the produce got to Broome it wasn't that fresh, but we looked forward to the ships coming anyway.

We had chooks and ducks, as did many households, and each day we fed them and collected the eggs. Water for our gardens was stored in forty-four-gallon drums. We'd go out and get cow manure from Four Mile, or the back of the meatworks, and soak it in the drums. As soon as we came home from school, our job was to scoop the water and pour it over the veggie patch. Although people were more concerned about their veggie patch than having a pretty front-yard, we still had beautiful gardens. Our front-yards had hibiscus plants, and trees such as frangipanis, oleanders, poincianas and golden showers. Most of the palm trees we grew were the ones that produced food, like coconut and date.

The houses that had mango trees usually belonged to the pearling masters and they would sell them. It cost a couple of pennies for one, which was expensive to us. Sometimes we would sneak in and try to shake the branches, or take what we could by poking long sticks through the fence and pulling them through the wire.

The Malay culture has influenced cooking in Broome more than any other. Lemongrass, garlic, ginger, chilli, tamarind, coconut, coriander, turmeric and other curry spices — all these flavours are found in the dishes made in our homes. Soya sauce is used a lot, and *belechan* (prawn paste), *ikan busu* (stinking fish) and chilli sambals are also common today. Rice came in from Singapore and we would eat it every day, sometimes more than once, and we would often have *nasi bubor* (rice porridge) for breakfast.

Some of the older Asians grew ginger and garlic and every house had *serai* (lemongrass). We called it 'fever grass' because it relieves fever. Our mothers would boil it up and we'd drink the water like tea.

Our parents would call out, '*Makan dulu*', and we knew it was time to come in, for a feed. The food we shared was mainly Malay food, like hot curry, chilli fish, chilli crab, mussels and pearl meat. There was no mercy. If you didn't eat curry, you starved.

selai or *ican selai*, is the little fish with a golden tail — a small, golden trevally. Another fish we loved as children was pumpkinhead which was used specially in soups. Butterfish, a big flat fish, was delicious fried. Both of these fish were caught in the fish traps down by the meatworks and are not often seen today.

Some families killed goats for meat because it was cheap. If they were Muslim, they killed it the Halal way. In this tradition animals must be slaughtered by draining the blood slowly, while prayers are said. Goats meat satays were popular for parties and if you wanted to buy goats meat, you drove out to Kanan (Fishermen's Bend) where it was sold.

Wedding parties would be celebrated at home rather than hiring a venue. If it was a Filipino wedding, the main food prepared was dinoguan, goats meat cooked in blood. The main food for a Malay wedding was goats meat satay and rendang, a beef or chicken curry cooked in coconut. For special celebrations, our family had chicken or duck, and turkey at Christmas. We also killed poultry the Halal way, and children would have the job of soaking the bird in hot water and plucking out the feathers.

We also used to salt meat (corned beef), a common practice throughout the Kimberley. Sometimes an aunty would come down from one of the stations near Derby and bring a lovely piece of corned beef for us. The only other beef we could afford was bones and oxtail for soup. We'd buy one shilling of soup bones and that would be the day's meat to feed us. At five in the morning, before Mum went to work, she would get up and cook our meal. When we came home from school for lunch there would be a pot of stew, soup bones, or fish soup and rice. We would heat it up on an old primus stove.

Most days Mum would order bread from W.E. Ellies who had a shop across the road from school. At lunchtime we would pick up the warm loaves with thick crusts to bring home. The loaves smelt so tempting that when we lived at the airport, we would often have eaten half of them by the time we got home. There was a small group of us and sometimes we'd pick on one person's bread. If mine had a big hole in it when I got home, I'd be in trouble.

'Oh no, not mine. I got into trouble yesterday, your turn today,' I'd say.

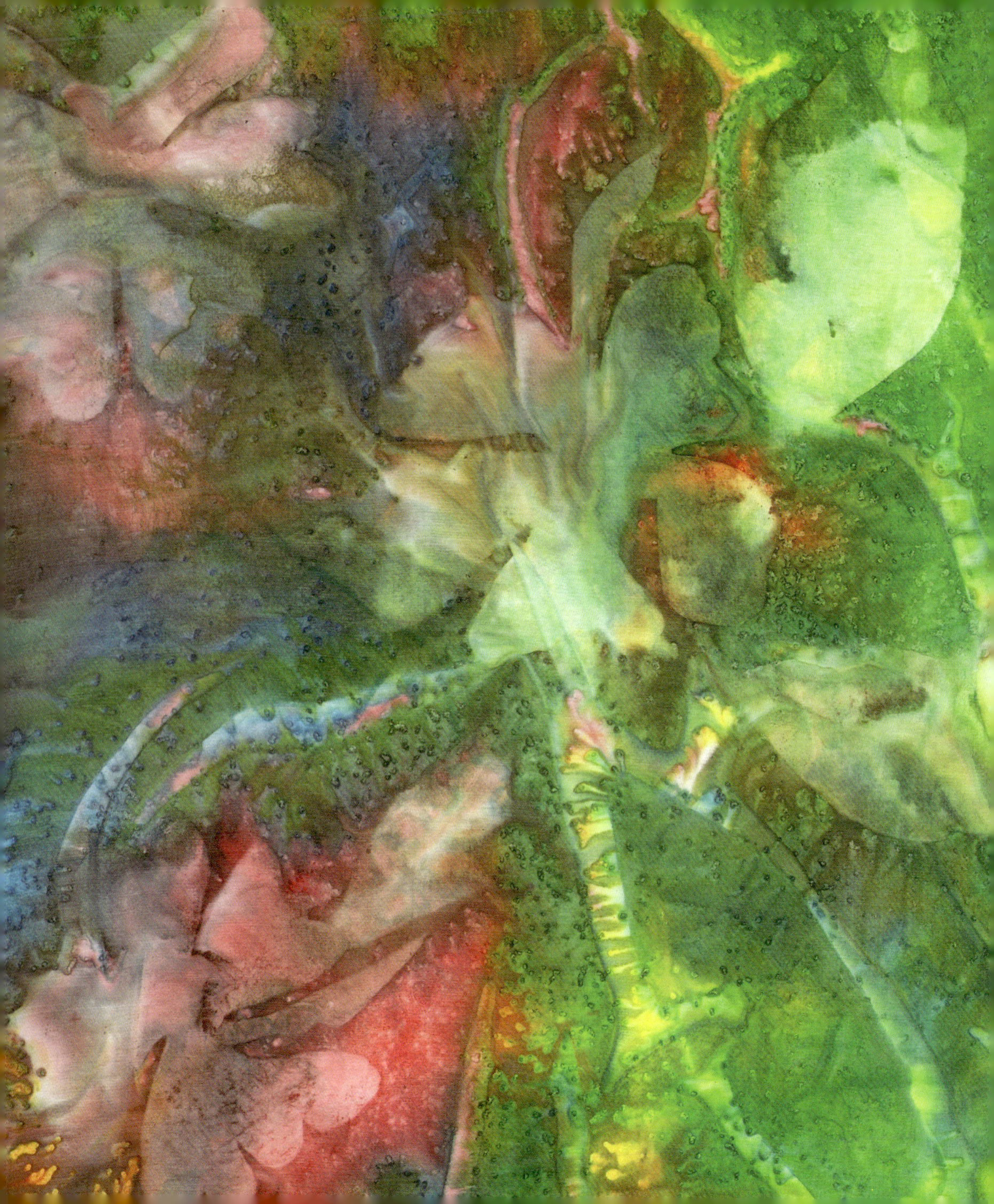

The moon and tides

We lived by the cycle of the moon, and the rhythm of the tides influenced much that happened in our lives. At the lowest ebb of a big tide we would walk for miles over the reef, and be amazed by the colours as we explored and collected food.

The high tides that occur at full moon and new moon, in fourteen-day cycles, are known as 'spring' tides. In Broome, the big 'king' tides are around March and November and nothing surpasses them. Three tides after full moon, the tide is the highest. The 'neap' tide is when there's not much tidal movement and the water is calm and glassy. I don't know which is better, the peace and tranquillity of the neaps or the colour and excitement of the big tides.

The lugger crews worked by the cycle of the moon, too. At

spring tide the water at sea was murky and so the boats anchored in nearby creeks. When their stores and water ran out, they came in and anchored at 'Streeter's Creek'. Diving was done on the neaps when the water was clear and calm.

Some people say full moon is best for getting fat crabs, and others prefer it when there is no moon. For a good feed, we would go out in the creeks and catch blue-hand crabs and mud crabs. We'd push wire down the crab holes and pull them out, claws clutching and scratching at the air as they fought to avoid becoming our supper.

When the sea flooded the town at king tide, it was a brilliant Ming blue. Like the house that Pearl was born in, many of the houses on the edge of Chinatown were built on high cement foundations, and at king tide they were like little islands. Uncle Jacob and Aunty Kay Sesar lived there, and we'd dive with their daughter, Aggie, and cousin, Betty, off their back steps. On those days the water would come right through to Sun Pictures, and it was something to see.

When Pearl and I played with the Chinatown Kids — Elsta and Louise Roe, Janet Rajak and Rosie Hunter — we paddled around the town in tin canoes made out of old sheets of iron. Some

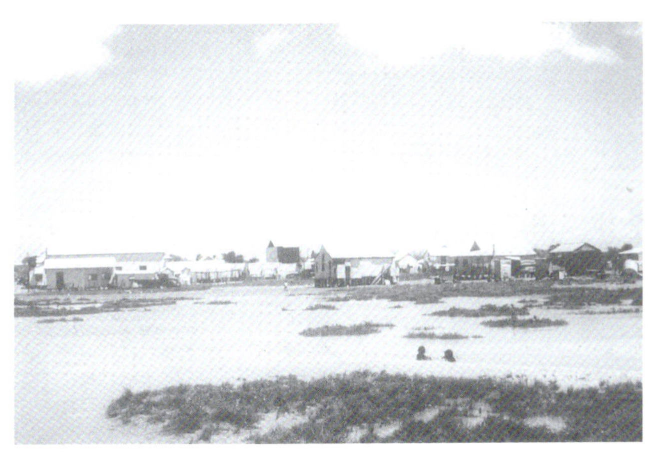

Swimming in Chinatown,
where we used to paddle our tin canoes.

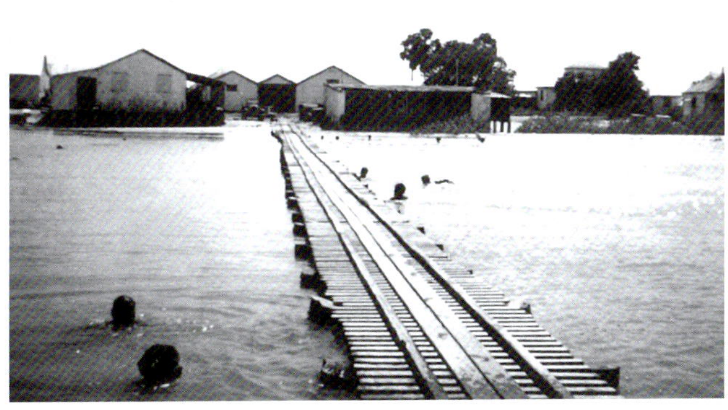

Streeter's Jetty, 1950s.

days we would swim out on the marsh and around the mangroves, diving off Streeter's Jetty and through the creeks. At other times we'd head for Bathing Shed Beach.

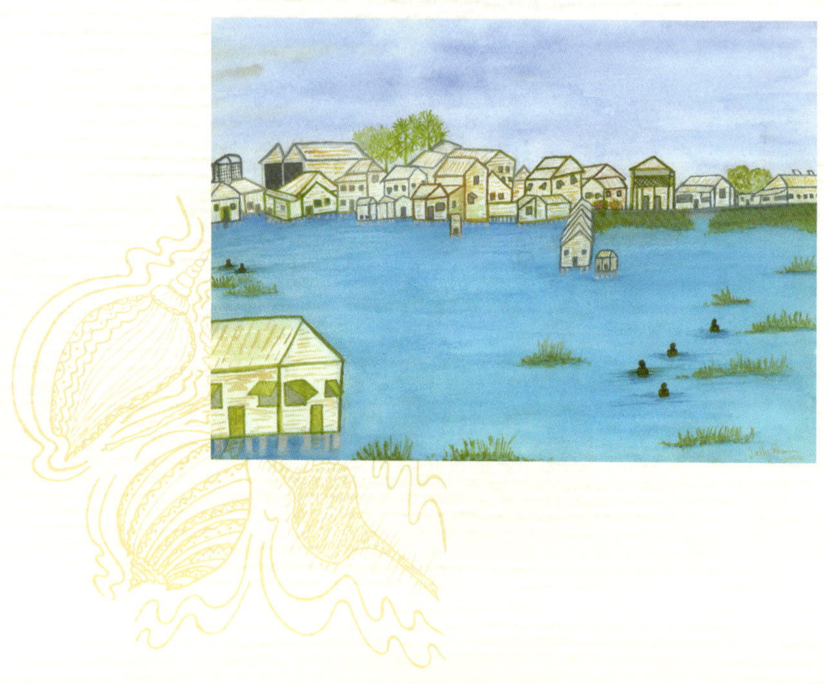

Fishing

After the war, there wasn't much money around, but we were fortunate because the bountiful seas provided most of our food. When the southeast winds blew, it was salmon season. The season would last from late April to early August, and just about everybody would drop what they were doing and head to the jetty.

The jetty was very long and narrow, and the cattle were herded on from the meatworks. The cattle rails began at the meatworks, and ran past the beach and onto the jetty. We were terrified that a bullock would jump over the rail so we would always play under the jetty. If there were no cattle around we would play on top, and when a train came past we would sing out 'train coming', and slip into the pockets along the side of the jetty until it had chugged past.

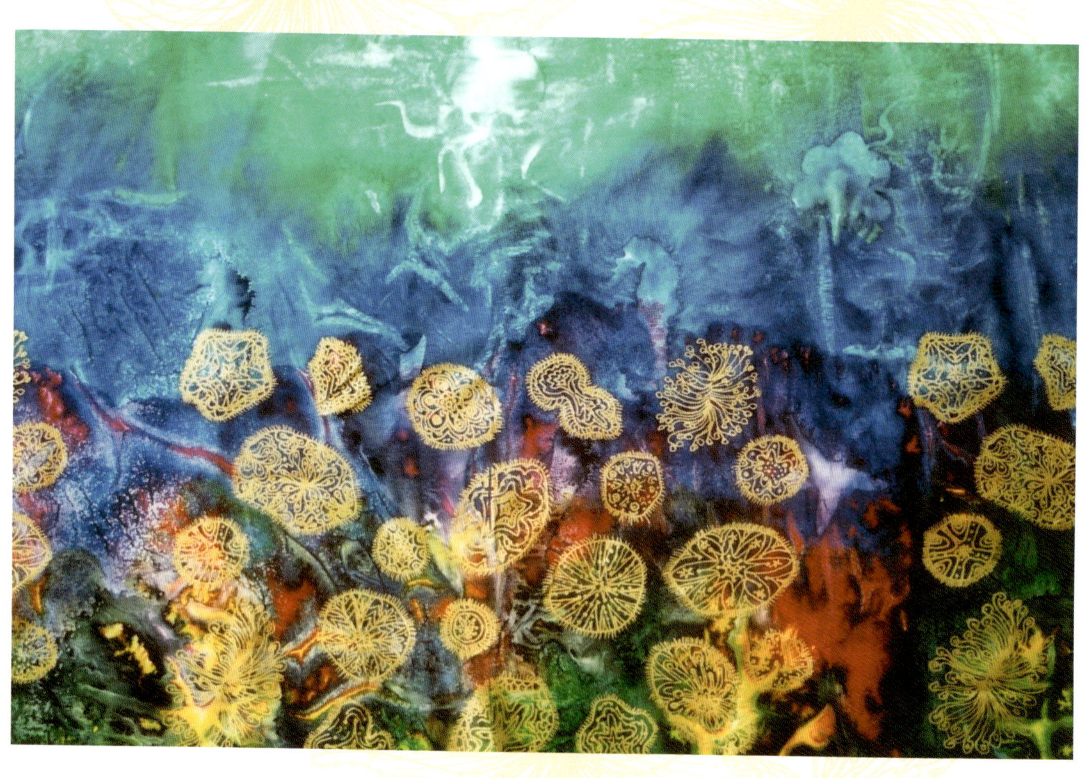

Sea Urchins

When the train was empty, we'd hop on the back and hitch a ride. The train used to run right along the bay to Chinatown.

During salmon season we could guarantee the old men like Horrie Miller, Willie Reid, Ah Ming and the old Aboriginal people who lived with the pearling families would be there. Everybody would be on the jetty with their lines in the water, and they would get the salmon when the tide was coming in and going out. We didn't use drag nets, but throw nets were used down on Bathing Shed Beach to get bait. Most families would fish with their hand lines, hooks, sinkers and bait. Believe it or not, we caught salmon using thread and cord, and we used rocks for sinkers with homemade hooks.

When we knew our mothers were fishing, we'd go straight from school to the jetty. If one of the woman caught a fish, we'd cook it on the coals down on the beach. I am sure nothing has ever tasted more delicious than a fresh salmon baked on the coals, and eaten with family and friends.

Most evenings we either played on the beach, or joined our family on the jetty. The adults would sit with their legs dangling over the side, but they always made sure the kids were sitting away from the edge. Roebuck Bay was famous for its sharks because of the blood and guts that ran into the sea from the meatworks' drain.

It was a quiet time, and a time for reflecting. If we got too noisy, the adults would shush us and we'd have to lower our voices. The soft blues, yellows and pinks of the evening sky softened the horizon, and the old people would tell us to sit quiet.

'Listen! Listen!' they'd tell us. 'Dugong singing.'

You could hear the plop of sinkers hitting the water and the swish of the lines as they flew through the air. At neap tide, when the ocean was like glass, you could see every ripple and fish jumping. Dugongs, porpoises, mantarays, sharks and salmon would fly and leap across the water. Sometimes you could hear dugongs and porpoises squeaking and crying.

We would take home enough fish to feed us for that day and then go back the next. We didn't have cars so we walked home, no matter how far it was. Before the season ended, families would salt as much salmon as they could to last a few months, and then wait until the southeast winds blew again.

There was something really special about fishing off the jetty. Maybe I could say that the best years of my life were spent fishing there with my family.

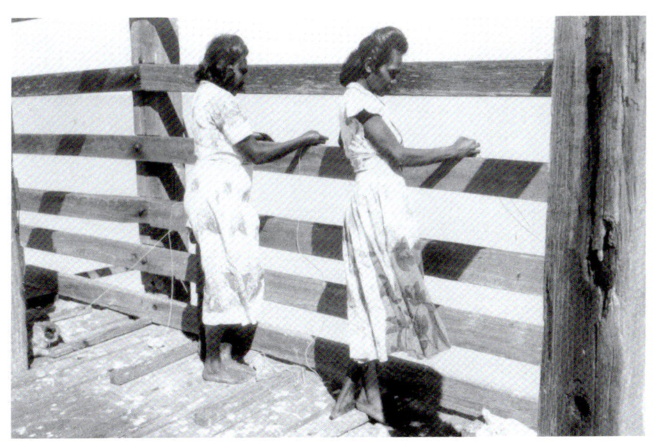

Jean Nicholas and Antonia Bernard fishing off the jetty, 1953.

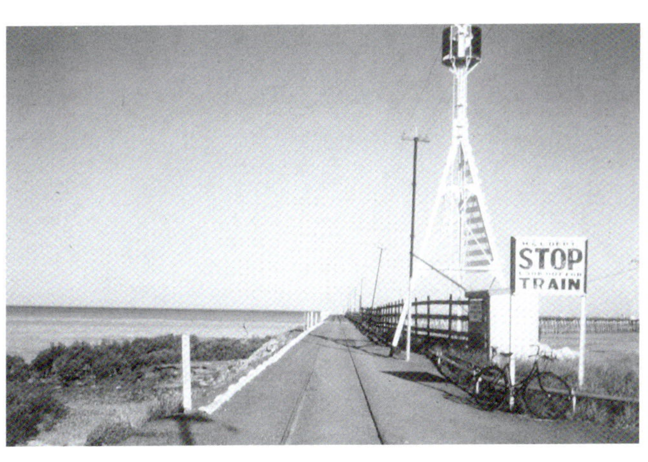

Broome Jetty, 1950s.

I can first remember fishing when I was about seven. Depending on the area in town where you lived, you would fishing in the closest creek. We'd cut up bonefish, *omong omong* (hermit crabs), pikes or long toms for bait. If we were hungry and didn't catch any fish we'd eat the bait! The hermit crabs would be scuttling all over the beaches, and they would leave long patterns in the sand. At night we would go out and collect a bucket, ready for the next day. *Manburr* (ghost crabs) would also make intricate patterns when the tide went out. These crabs would roll up little balls of sand around their burrows. We loved chasing them around in the evenings on low tide.

We also used to fish off the meatworks' drain while we were waiting for the tide to go out. We'd walk out along the pipe into the water and fish from the end. We hardly ever had fishing lines — the boys would make bamboo rods and we'd use crochet cotton for our lines. Sometimes we used bent needles and safety-pins for hooks. We would always be extra careful and look out for each other to make sure there were no sharks hanging around.

Around September the season for reef fish began, and everyone would be oystering, shelling, cockling and fishing for blue bone, snapper or cod. The tides would tell us what to do. On the October and November king tides we'd be out on the reefs or collecting cockles in the mud. If we wanted *berga berga* (sand mussels) for supper, we'd head down to Magistrate's Beach or Red Cliff (out the front of Roebuck Bay Caravan Park), and collect a bucket of them. They were delicious boiled up with lemongrass.

When the march flies were biting, people would say that meant *jinup* (stingray), oysters and bluebone and other reef fish were ready to eat. If the oysters were fat, the jinup were fat and that's when the boys went to spear them. Jinup is a real delicacy, especially when it's partly cooked on the coals, and the fat is where the taste is.

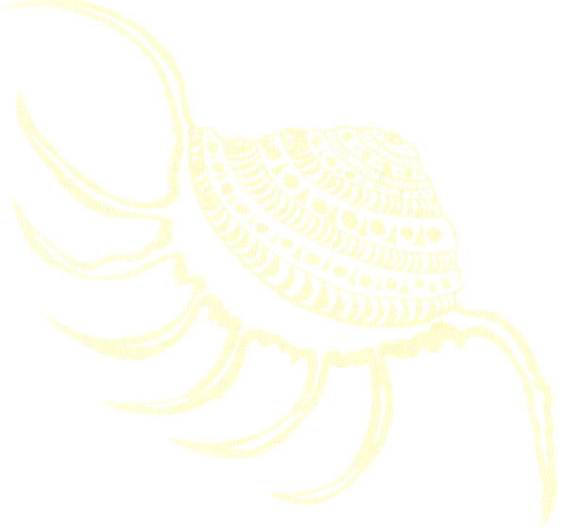

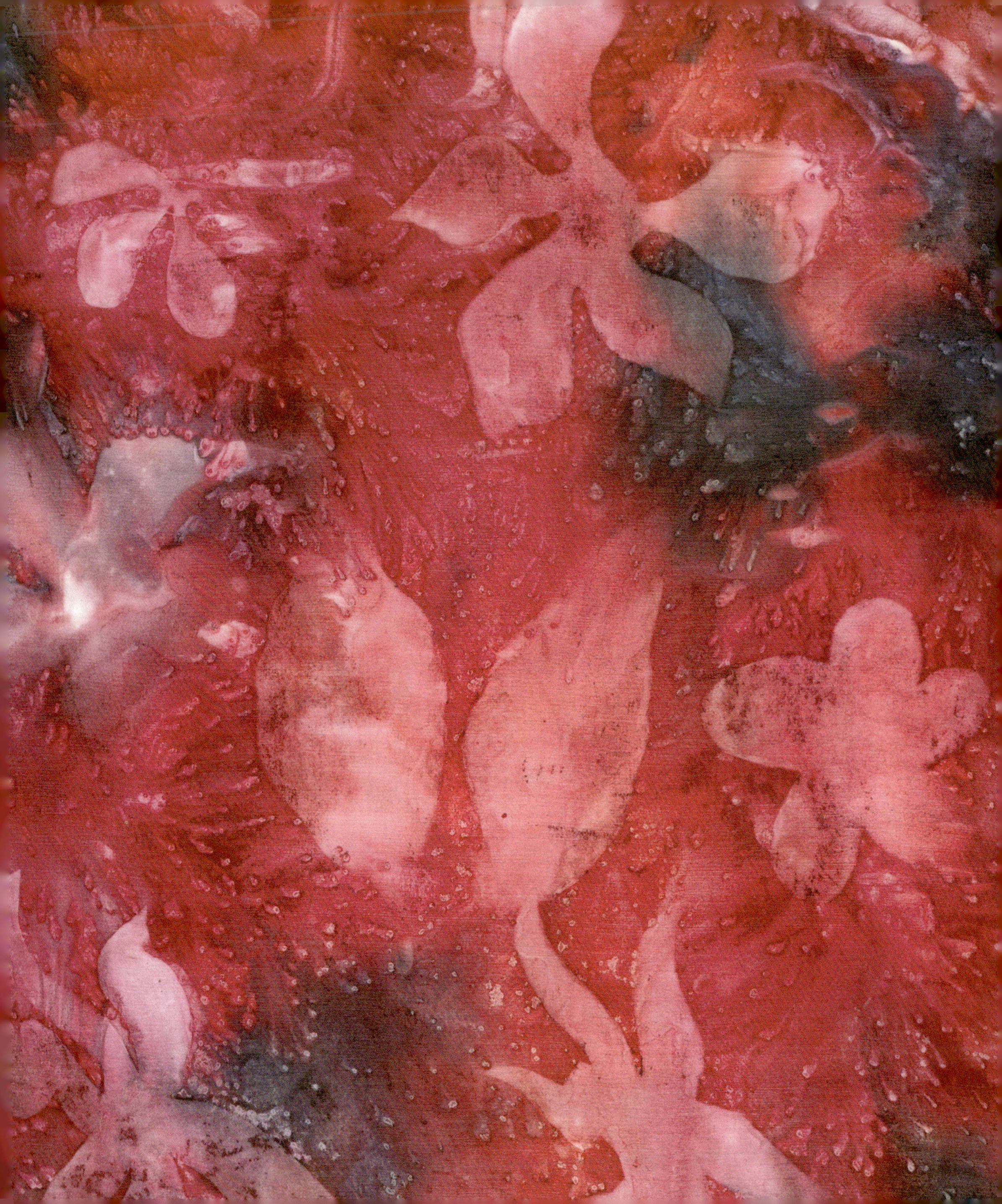

Redell Beach

Redell Beach was one of my favourite places. When the tide was full we'd swim till we were black and wrinkly, and when the tide was out we'd spend the day exploring the reef and looking for treasures — you couldn't beat it. Years ago we would find cowries and rare shells of all kinds, some dry and washed up, and many alive. There was coral in every colour. Now it's muddy and you are lucky to find anything.

The West Australian State Ships, like the *Koolinda* and the *Koolama*, would travel along the coast bringing passengers and supplies to the towns in the northwest, and they would sometimes come close to the reef. On the king tides, the crew would throw apples and oranges into the water for any children who were shelling or fishing out on the exposed reef. It wasn't unusual to see bits of debris from the ships floating by.

I remember once it was a holiday and we were all at Redell Beach with the nuns. It was low tide and an elderly nun, Mother Angela, was walking on the reef with us. Suddenly she stopped and called out for us to come and see what she had found.

'Beautiful green coral,' she cried.

We all raced over the reef to discover that the 'beautiful green coral' was a cabbage that had been washed ashore! Needless to say, from that day on, her nickname was 'Green Coral'.

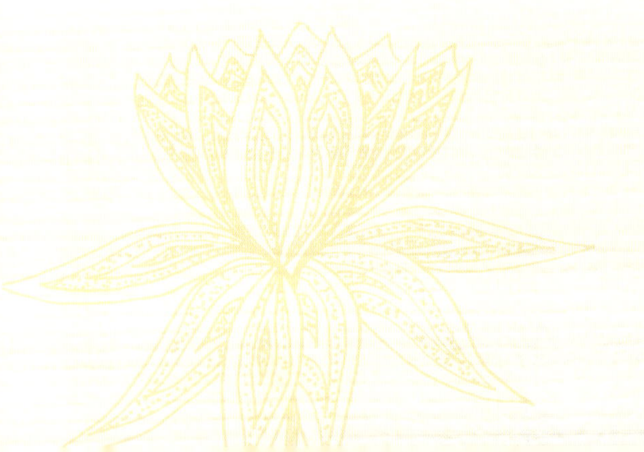

Picnics

Some Sundays, when Mum had a day off, she would organise a taxi and we would drive out to Quarantine Hills (the Port of Broome) and have wonderful picnics. There were only a few buildings out there. The Quarantine Station vetted all of the overseas boats, and if the crew or the cargo were suspected of contamination they were kept until cleared. The authorities were frightened of leprosy, smallpox and tuberculosis.

It used to be very picturesque out there, with the white sandhills, red cliffs and clear turquoise water. We would camp under the trees and spend the day fishing and swimming. If you look there now, the dunes have been flattened and there is a huge silo and fuel tanks, and of course, the big wharf.

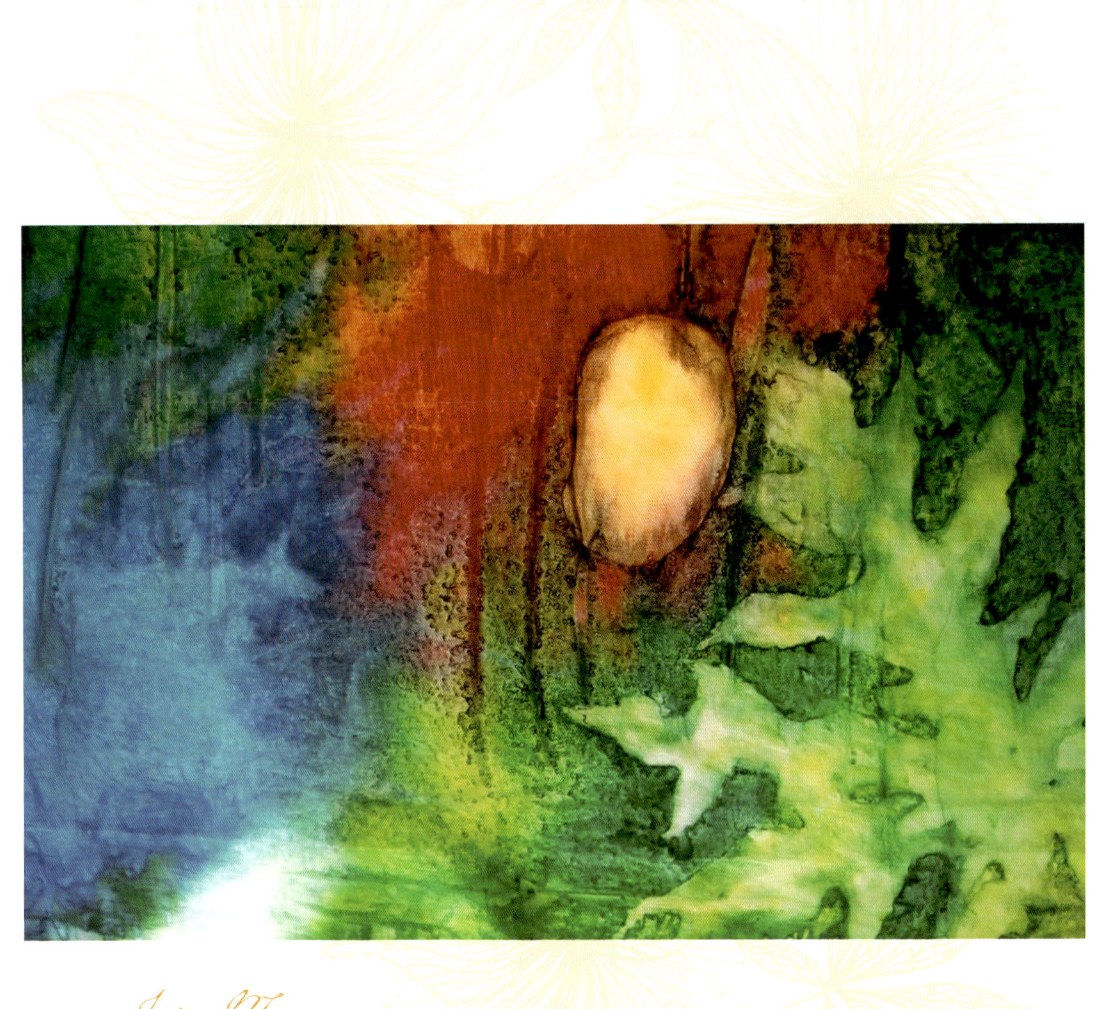

Juicy Mangoes

At Willie Creek, the luggers used to hide in the protected lagoon when 'willy-willies' or cyclones were coming, which is probably how Willie Creek got its name. *Gulgurin* (little twisters) were common and would blow through the town. We'd run and hide from the strong, noisy spirals of wind which would be full of red dust, leaves, paper and all sorts of things.

The Corpus family had planted poinciana trees at Willie Creek, and we would head out there with the orphanage girls on the back of one of Mr Pryor's trucks. To get there, we would travel over the marsh through Denim Station, owned by Mr Denim. He also owned the butcher's shop in Chinatown.

For lunch we'd have camp pie and bread, but you could always rely on catching fish and grilling them on the coals. We'd also cook periwinkles and snails. There was no sign of crocodiles back then.

On the way home, we'd be so tired that we would huddle up together with the little ones safely tucked in the middle, and the older girls dangling their legs over the back. Of course the road was bumpy and full of potholes, and occasionally someone would go over the edge.

There were only a few coloured families who owned cars — Broome had very few bicycles, let alone cars — and if you were lucky you had one bike in a family. If the family next door didn't have one, they'd come and borrow your bike to go downtown.

The Rahmans, Bin Salliks and Nassers had their vehicles to deliver fish, and Uncle Vincent Martin, who was married to my godmother, Aunty Gracie (Ursula), also had a car. They would sometimes take Pearl and I for a weekend outing, if Mum was at work.

Although Anawei and Willie Reid couldn't drive, they both owned old jalopies — utilities that were quite low to the ground — and occasionally we used them for picnics. We got to go because Uncle Ben Mathews and Uncle Jacob Sesar were the drivers. If we went up the coast we would have that many punctures along the way, it would take us just about a whole day to get out there. If we got bogged, we would have to put down grass and leaves to get the car out. It was always great fun and we'd fish and swim until it was time to jolt back to Broome. Occasionally, we would encounter dingoes on the way home, and some were cheeky enough to chase the jalopies.

Our mothers would yell, 'Put your legs in!'

We counted sixteen one night along the road coming back from Barred Creek. Now, you are lucky to see one.

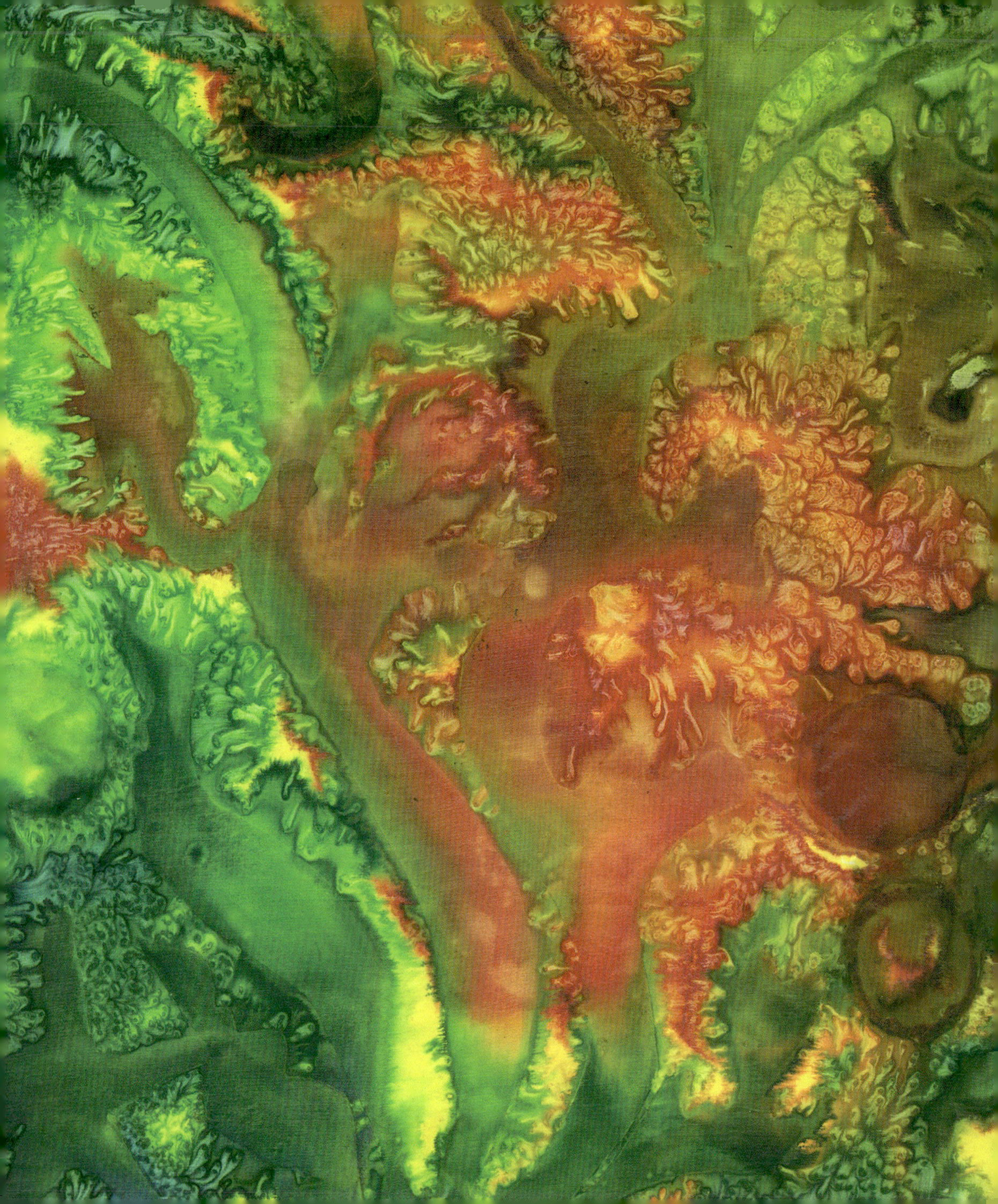

Moving

When I was a child we moved house many times. I was seven when we shifted from the Long House to another big house on the corner of Barker and Walcott Streets, owned by Ali Rahman and his family. Our family had the side verandah and we used to enter the house from Walcott Street. There were separate entrances for each of the families.

The year before, I had gone to my first ever wedding — a double wedding for the Rahman sisters, Una and Hasma. They both married Muslim men and the service was held in the Catholic Presbytery. That wedding was my first big party, and I was in a state of wonderment at the beauty of Una and Hasma.

Ali Bin Salleh, from Singapore, married Hasma. Frances

Salawatoe, from Koepang in Timor, wed Una. We were able to live in the house because Ali was Simeon's friend and countryman. We shared the bathroom and kitchen, and ate our meals together. The year we stayed with them, Una and Frances had a daughter, Halimah, and Hasma and Ali had a son, Johnny.

We soon moved with Hasma, Ali and baby Johnny, along Walcott Street to a house near the airport. We had to carry most of our belongings, and the larger pieces were taken on the old jalopy.

There's a funny story about moving. Aunty Bella was always petrified of dogs. She came over from the orphanage to help us shift, and she was given little Johnny to carry. As we traipsed down the street, a dog came out barking and we all just kept walking. But not Aunty Bella! She screamed and shrieked, and of course the dog went straight up to her.

'Aunty Bella! Aunty Bella! The baby!' we all shouted.

But no, instead of holding the baby up high and protecting him, she used him like a shield as if to say, 'Take the baby, not me.' With all the screaming, shouting and crying, the dog took off in fright.

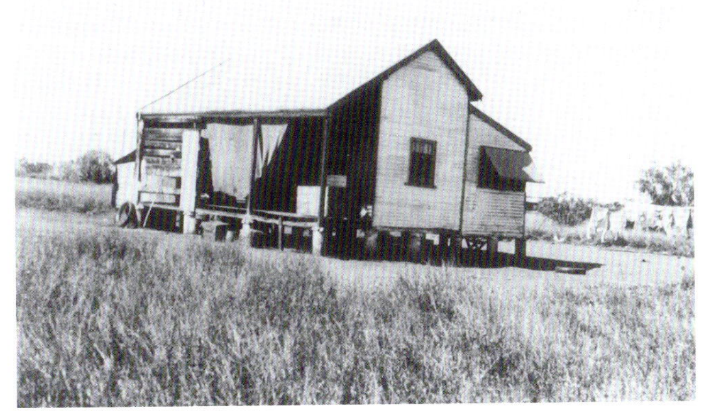

The airport house,
many years before we lived in it.

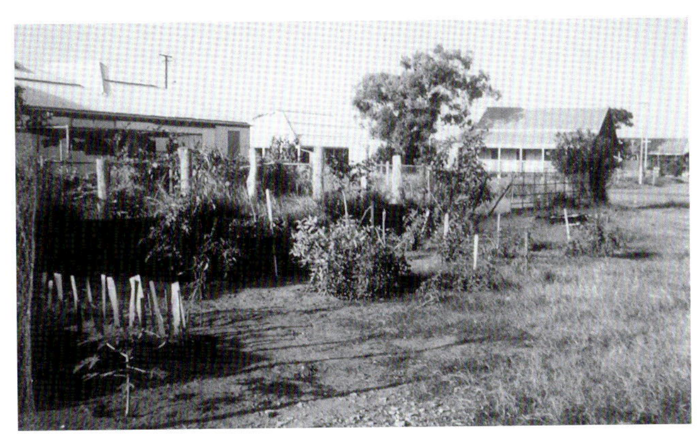

Our vegetable garden — across the road
you can see Ellies' Store, St Mary's School
and kindergarten, Robinson Street.

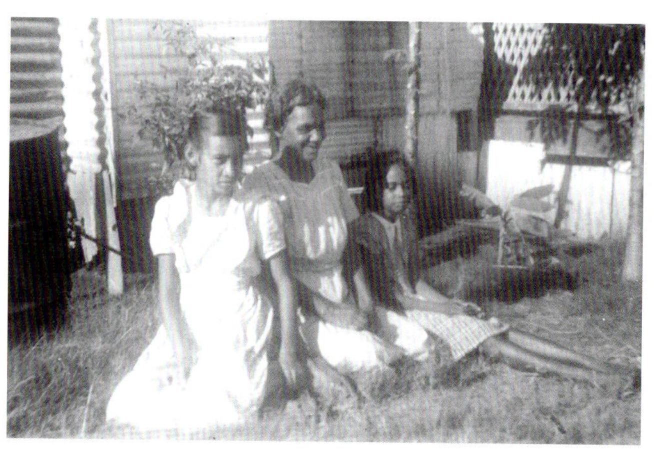

With Pearl and Aunty Bella,
Robinson Street, c1951.

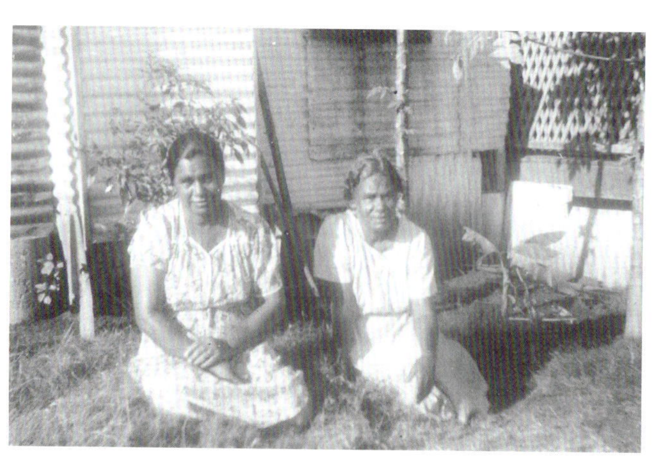

Mum and Aunty Bella,
Robinson Street, c1951.

The airport house was the smallest house I had ever lived in. It was owned by two Malay men, one lived in Darwin and the other, Hussan, lived on the back verandah near the small kitchen. Hasma and Ali's little family had the middle room, and we slept out on the front verandah. This time the verandah was small, with timber poles holding up the canvas roof. If it rained from the wrong direction, we would get soaked and would have to move inside. We stayed together with Hasma and Ali until their daughter, Diane, was born and then, sadly for us, they moved to Darwin.

The second house we lived in on Robinson Street, we rented from the Ellies family. It was the first time we had lived in a house by ourselves. There was just Mum, Pearl, myself and Simeon, when he was in from the sea. It was another large Broome house with wide verandahs, shutters and lattice. It was old and in need of a good paint, and the roof and lattice needed replacing. We all slept, beds lined up in the sleepout, with mosquito nets dropping down from the rafters. It was just over the road from St Mary's School and had no fence, so it was often a thoroughfare for families living behind us. They would greet us night or day as they passed by. Well, it was only courtesy, since they were cutting through our yard. You can imagine how some of these greetings developed into lengthy visits, animals and all.

I was old enough to do chores by then and at dinner time, Pearl and I would have to set and clear the table, and take turns to wash up or wipe. Sometimes there'd be fights when we forgot whose turn it was.

Every morning at about six, we also took turns to do morning chores. One of us would ride the bike to get ice from the ice factory on the corner of Walcott and Saville Streets, and the other one would walk to Chinatown to get meat from the butcher. It was always good when we had fish at home because then one of us would have one less chore. At home we had a small icebox to keep butter and water cool, and if you were lucky the ice would last about a day. We'd carry a hessian sack to put the block of ice in, and then ride like mad straight home.

We had a huge brick stove, and in winter we would sit by the stove and toast our bread on a fork or stick. It used to be *that* cold. I hated that stove because Pearl and I had to clean out the grate. If we didn't clean it regularly, the ashes would build up and we would be covered in soot. I used to feel like Cinderella.

Aunties

When the girls at the orphanage were old enough, it was time for them to go and work in Broome or other communities. We were still living in Robinson Street, and sometimes Mum took in some of the girls that had nowhere to go. They were my mother's kin and they shared a special bond with her because their mothers, who had passed away, had also come from Halls Creek. These young women all took on jobs at the hospital, working as nurses or ward maids.

I would often look at them in awe, especially when they were dressed up to go out, or to work. Their outfits were tailored with padded shoulders and heels. Handbags were also an essential accessory. Their hairstyles were in the early fifties fashion, the likes of pageboys, kiss curls, perms, French knots and hairnets. Pearl and

I would sit and watch them putting on their make-up — eyebrow pencil, lipstick and rouge, as well as the unforgettable scents of 'Goya' and 'Evening Paris'. As soon as they left we couldn't wait to put the make-up on ourselves.

We also had aunties coming to stay with us from throughout the Kimberley and as far away as the Pilbara and Northern Territory. Most of them were from the stolen generation and had originally been taken from the Halls Creek area. They were all half-caste women and would call each other *jija* (sister). Sometimes they would stay for weeks. It was the old girls' time to reminisce about the mission days. Sitting on wide verandahs in deck chairs, on hot summer nights under the stars, they would talk for hours. Pearl and I loved listening to them talk about country and hear stories about the tricks they used to play on each other.

Aunty Topsy O'Meara was one of our favourite aunties, and even hearing her laugh would make us kids bust out laughing. When they were children living at Beagle Bay, her and Aunty Bella and Aunty Margaret were known for their pranks. One time, when the other girls were asleep, they tied pieces of string to the girls' ankles and to the handles of their toilet pans. When the girls stirred in their sleep, they spilled the contents of the pans and made an awful mess.

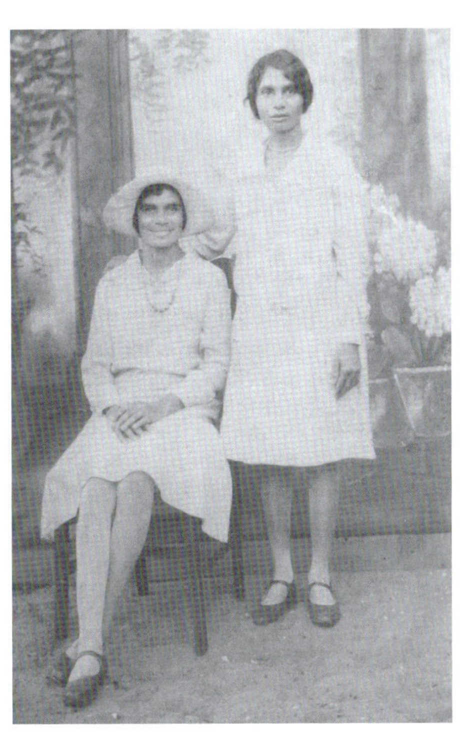

Mum with Aunty Laura at Murakami's Photo Studio, Chinatown, c1920s.

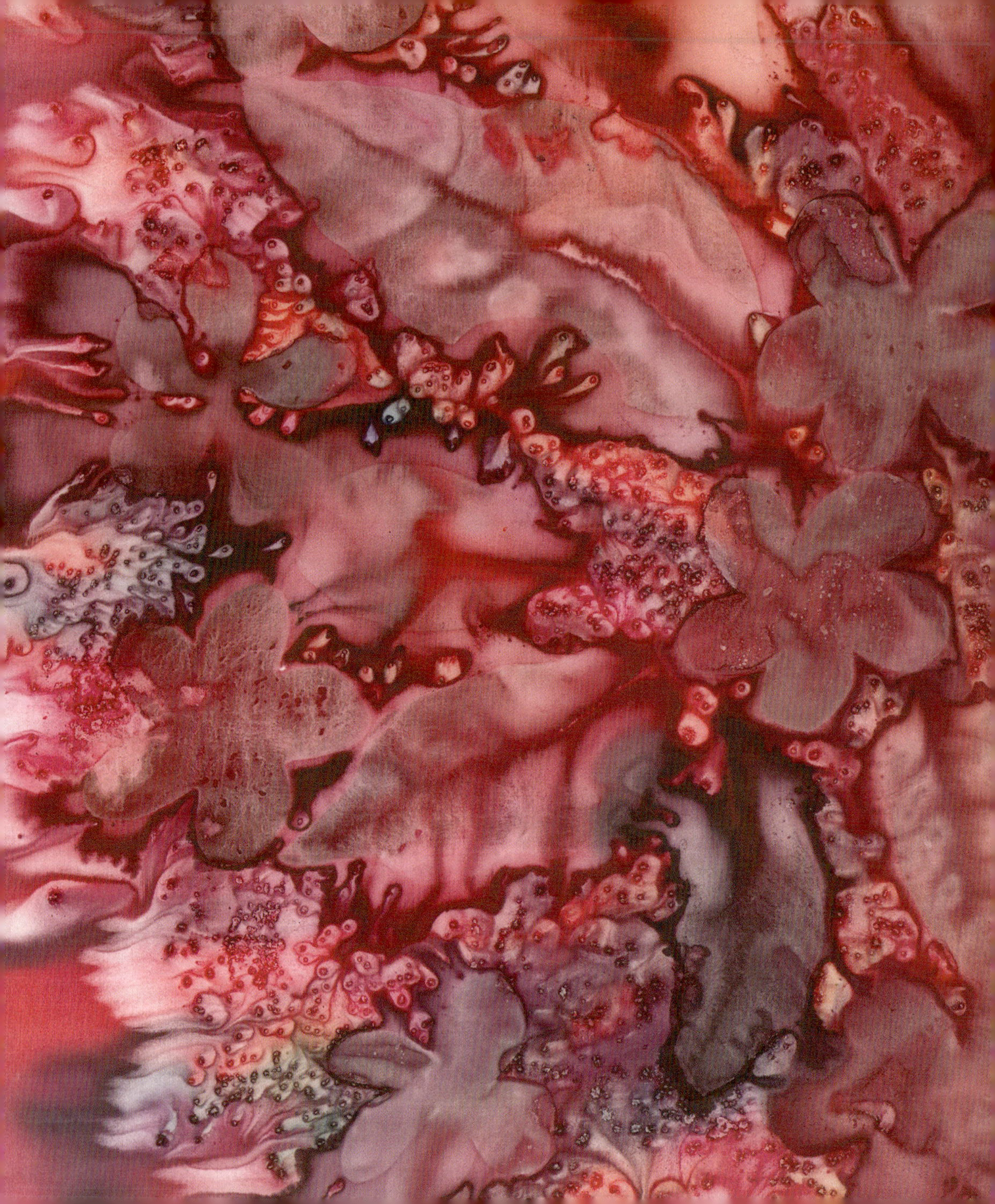

The Airport Kids

Moving close to the airport was like moving to a different suburb. Because we had to walk everywhere we usually played near to where we lived, and so I mixed with the Airport Kids, who were mostly my relations. Around town there were the 'Airport Kids', the 'Chinatown Kids' and the 'Up-the-hill Kids' (Kennedy Hill).

My closest friends were Mary-Rose Lee, Doris Mathews, Yvonne Martin and Maureen Howard, and we hung out together all the time. The older girls did their own thing, and Pearl played with Mary-Anne Martin and Eileen Matsumoto.

The boys also played an important role in our games and there would be plenty of challenges between us. Danny Howard, Brian Lee, Terry Mathews, Phillip Matsumoto, Alec Howard and

Kenny Dean were always around, and sometimes we joined up with Mervyn and Owen Torres. Cas Torres, Ronnie Howard and Mickey Mathews were a bit older than the others, but they would often be close by to make sure that we didn't get into too much trouble.

Before the war, there must have been Japanese houses with Japanese gardens over the road from our house because there were beautiful ponds that would fill up with water when the rains came. In the rainy season, they would be teeming with hundreds of tadpoles which we'd collect in jars. Behind our place was the Martin's house. They had a pond graced by two imposing palm trees, and we called it our swimming pool.

Now that we were Airport Kids, our main playground was the marsh and the mangroves. We would wander along the mangroves, especially when it was a king tide, and the sun would burn down on our heads. When it got too hot, we would cool off in the huge sea that formed over the mudflats and surrounded the town. Sometimes when we came home for lunch and saw the blue water at our doorstep, we'd race into it and spend the afternoon diving and swimming. School would be long forgotten.

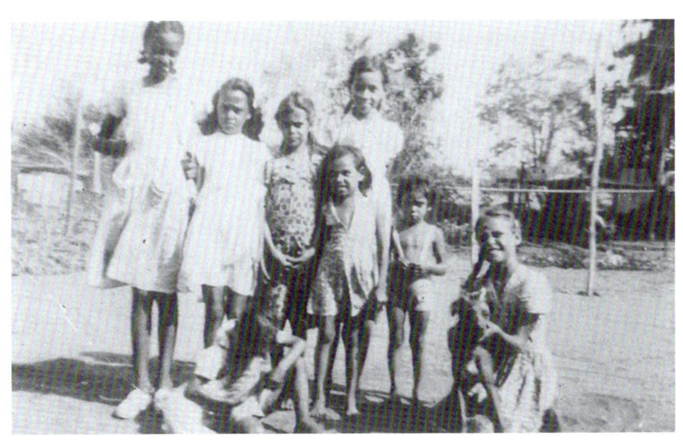

The airport kids — ltor: Julie Mamid, Pauline Mamid (dec), Yvonne Martin, Margaret Howard (dec), Pearl, Doreen Howard (dec), and Mary Anne Martin. I am not sure who the child is sitting on the ground in front.

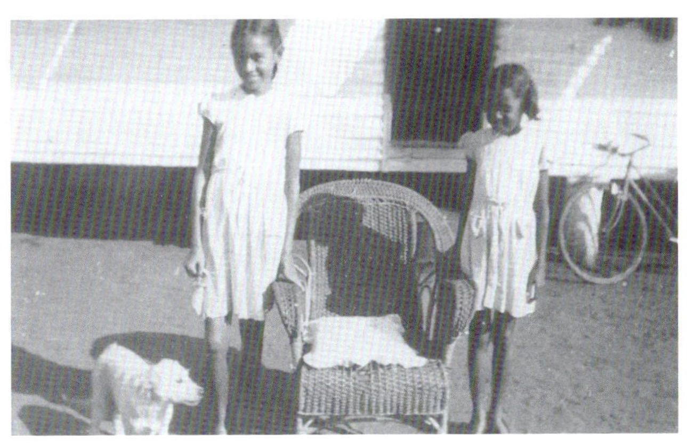

With Pearl and our dog, Johnny, at the airport house, c1948.

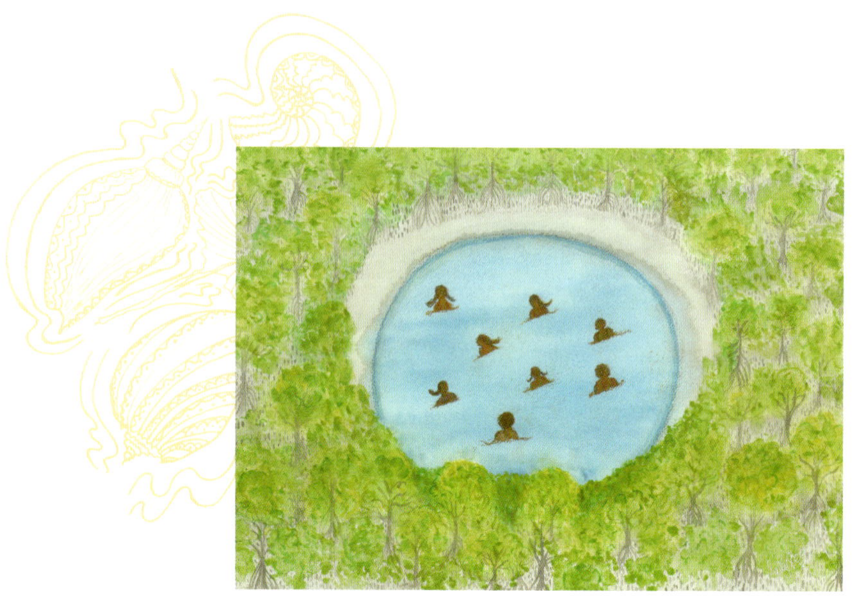

There was a bomb crater near the airport which we used to swim in. We kept it a secret from the other kids around town, but apparently there were other bomb holes, We couldn't believe our luck when the tide would come in and fill it, and there was a ready-made swimming pool. The bomb hole would top up with water every spring tide and so it was there whenever we wanted to go for a swim. During spring tide, it was so tempting you couldn't help but go for a swim, and we often missed a couple of days of school.

At the bomb hole we swam and dived and did all sorts of tricks. We skated across the soft mud, rolled around it and slid into the hole. Then we'd head to Pulling Creek (at the back of Paspaley

Shopping Centre and Morgan's Camp), which only flowed in one direction, and we'd float to Morgan's Creek and on to Streeter's Jetty.

We also played a lot around Herbert Street. One of the planes that had been shot down during the war was lying on the corner of Frederick and Herbert Streets. It was in good shape with no rust, and the instrument panels and seats intact. It was perfect for playing air hostesses, pilots and passengers.

We were always jumping into the abandoned air-raid shelters around Herbert Street and near the airport. We would be the Americans or French against the Germans — we never played war against the Japanese. The Americans were our heroes, and we wanted to be them — shooting the Germans, like cowboys shooting the Indians. If we knew then what we know now, we would have wondered who the good guys really were. The shelters were quite long, and it was lucky nobody fell in and broke a leg because there were no markers, just trenches in the ground. When we climbed down into them, the walls would come up to our heads — maybe four foot high.

There was live ammunition around too, and the boys would open the shells and tip out the powder. We would light up the gunpowder and wait for the noise. I don't know how we didn't get killed! When we got tired of playing war games, we'd go back to cowboys and Indians and throw things across the trenches at each other.

Another favourite game around the airport was swinging like Tarzan, branch to branch, from tamarind tree to tamarind tree. The boys would yell, 'Race you to the top!' and away they'd go. We'd have to be the judges. Us girls would cheer them on, never having a clue who won because we stayed safely on the ground!

Although we usually stayed close to home, the whole of Broome was really like our backyard. Kennedy Hill was a great place to play. It was one of the only hills in Broome, and we'd climb to the top and slide down on pieces of cardboard or sheet iron.

Marbles we would play anywhere, especially at the corner of intersections. It was a major drawcard to bring kids together.

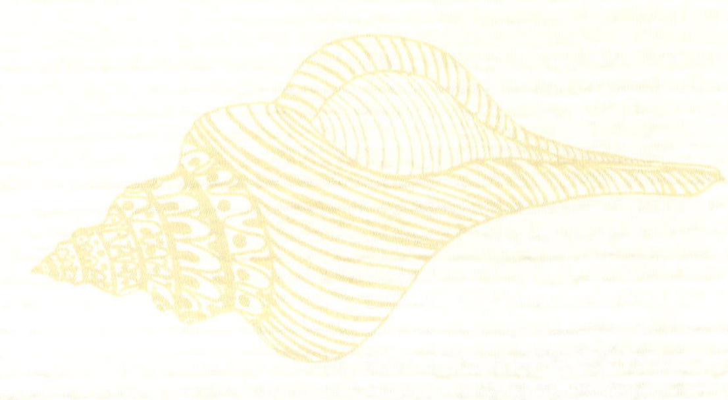

Shark Attack

It was a life of swimming, although none of us were ever taught to swim. We spent hours and hours each day in water full of sharks and sea snakes, and maybe even crocodiles — well, we never saw crocodiles. People just assumed there were crocs at Streeter's Jetty.

We did see lots of sea snakes, although I don't remember anyone ever telling us they were deadly. The big ones with the fins and the tail were everywhere, and we would often swim amongst the little bandy bandys. Sharks were common at the jetty, but we never saw any in the creeks or mangroves.

Bathing Shed Beach, one of our favourite swimming spots, was surrounded by a ten-foot-high shark fence. We loved to swim out to the deep end of the fence, which would be covered on big tides, and dare each other to stand or sit on it.

In the late 1940s, Mrs Maxwell, the wife of the train driver, was sitting on the beach one day reading a book when she saw a woman swimming with her fiancé outside the fence. Suddenly there was a commotion in the water and she saw a shark attacking the woman. Mrs Maxwell was the only person on the beach and she quickly swam out to help. There was a tug of war, with the fiancé and Mrs Maxwell pulling one way and the shark the other, but the shark ended up taking the woman's left arm. They said there was a reward for whoever caught the shark, and for weeks afterwards we used to go fishing off the jetty. Eventually someone did get the shark with the arm and the engagement ring.

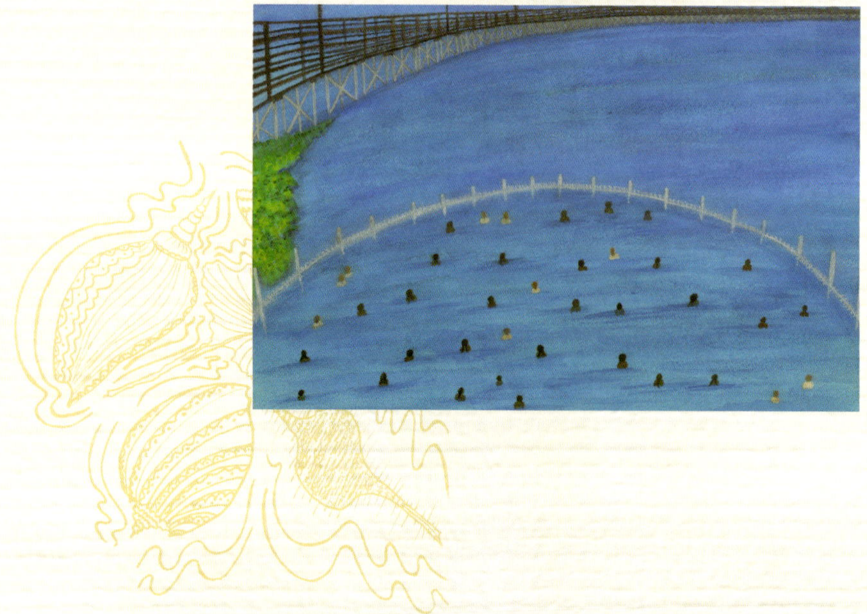

Fish Traps

There were many Filipino men working on the luggers, and there are still remnants of some of the Filipino fish traps down near where the meatworks used to be. One ran straight out from where the caravan park is today. It belonged to Tio Dalmatio. 'Tio' means 'uncle' in Filipino. The other was further along from the meatworks about five hundred metres away, and was cared for by Tio Lorenzo. Tio Benato cared for another trap further up the beach. You can see the posts in the mudflats today.

To us children, the fish traps seemed big and very long. When the tide was out, we would walk onto the mudflats to see the fish caught in pools of water within the pockets of the trap. We'd go and help Tio Dalmatio get out his catch when he was clearing his trap. It was important to move fast to beat the incoming tide, and be the first one into town to sell the fish. Tio Dalmatio was on his own and didn't have a car, so sometimes the boys would go down after school and help him. Like a few of the other old Filipino men, Tio Dalmatio was looked after by the Puertollano family. Stan and Elizabeth Puertollano would help to sell his fish around town, and a few years down the track Stan had his own fish trap across the bay with Henry Corpus.

After the war most of the traps were owned by Malays, but looked after by the Filipinos. These Malay families had cars and utility trucks. Aunty Biddy Bin Sallik owned one of the traps and after it was cleared, she would drive around and stop at every door and sell the fish. The Rahmans and the Nassers also owned traps and we would often hitch a ride on their trucks and drive around town while they sold their catch.

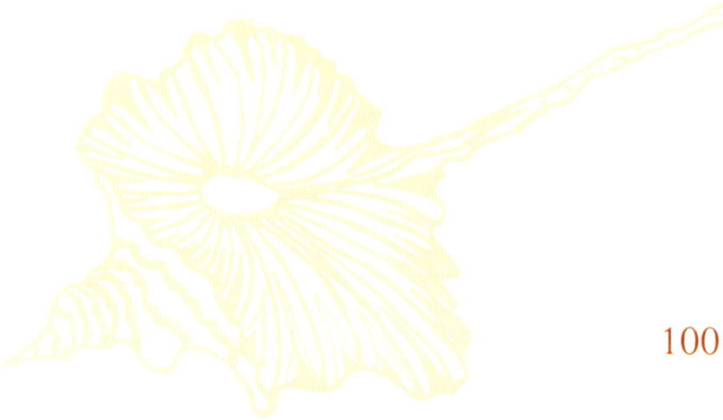

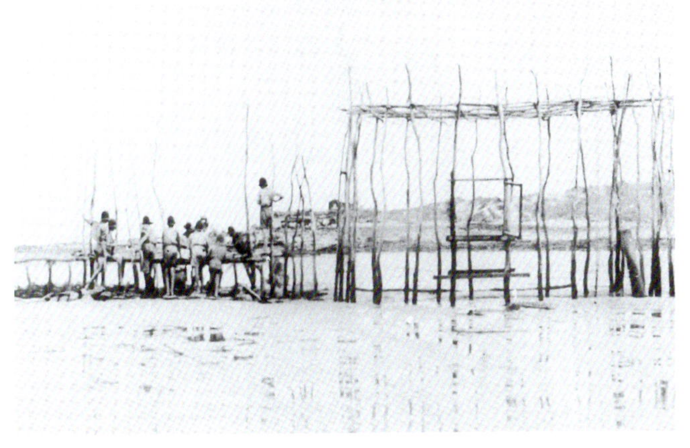

Building a fish trap at Meatworks Beach before the war.

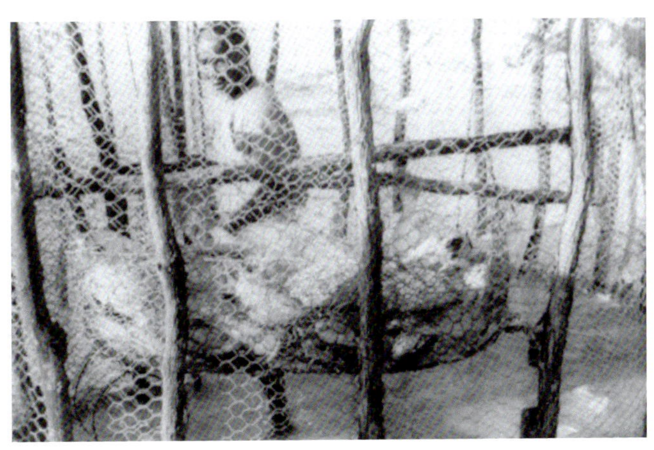

Tio Lorenzo gathering fish in his trap at low tide, 1950.

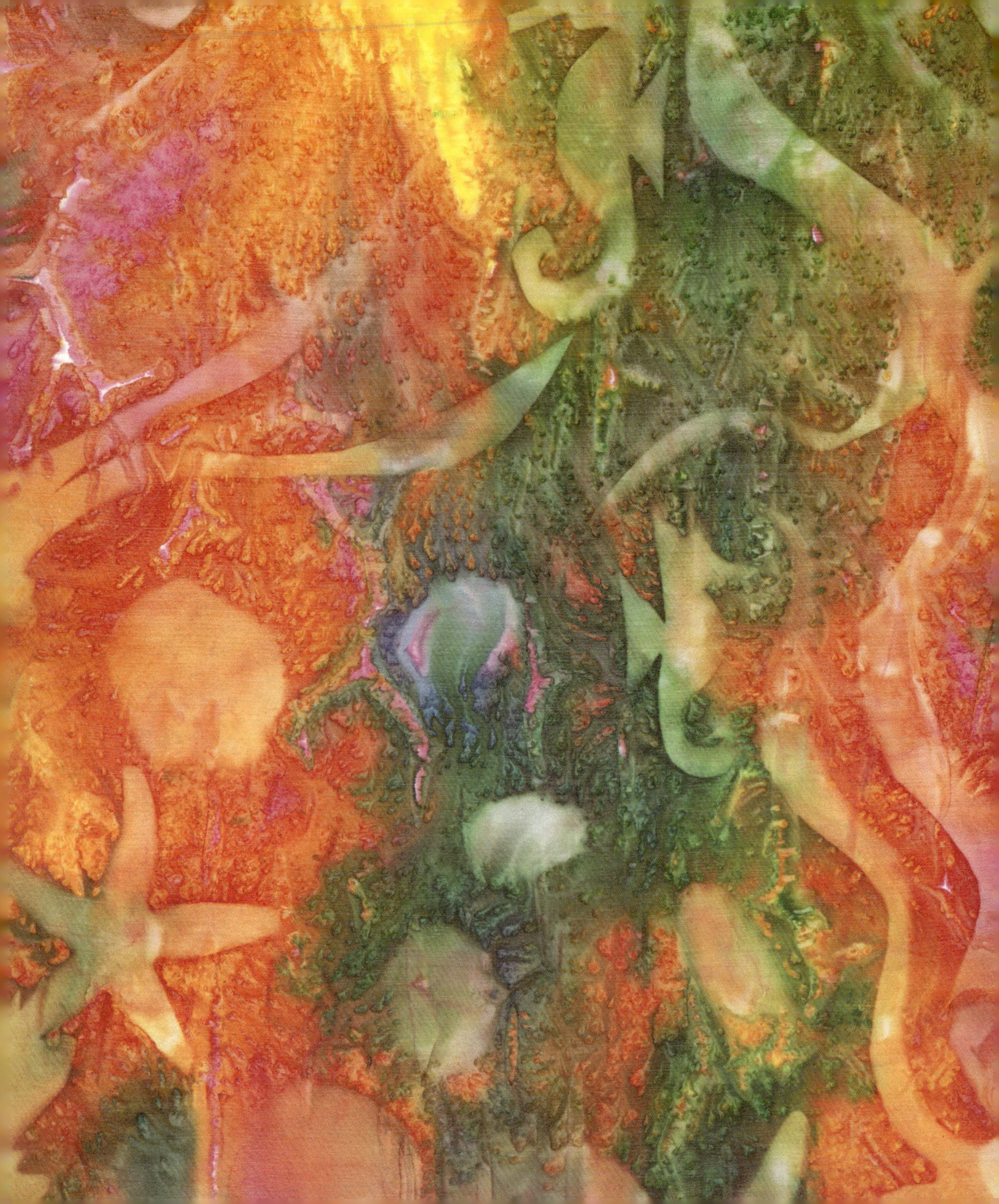

Chinatown

One of my earliest memories of Chinatown was walking with my mother to the Commonwealth Bank on the corner of Hamersley and Frederick Streets, and lining up to get coupons — one week we could get food and the next we could get clothing. Usually I would get clothes when Pearl grew out of them, but sometimes Mum would get material from Fong Sam's or Tack's. Most of my aunties were good dressmakers and did their sewing on treadle machines.

Shop food was short in those post-war years, and coupons were the way families did their shopping; they used to come in a little booklet. We collected the coupons from the bank and then we'd go to the butchers or the grocers. Because we could only get groceries on one week, we had to ration to make it through the fortnight. I remember 'Big Sister' tinned butter. We used to spread it sparsely on our bread. We had dripping on our bread too, it was *that* tasty.

In town all the roads were dirt except the three main streets — Hamersley, Weld and Robinson. Even Chinatown didn't have bitumen, it was grey sand full of shell grit. There were some beautiful trees though, and in Carnarvon Street there were golden showers and poincianas. Near Streeters and along Dampier Terrace there were majestic boabs.

It was only in Chinatown where you saw bars on the shops and houses. At home we never worried about locking up because nobody broke into people's homes. We left everything open — our doors and windows and our big shutters, even when we went to the pictures. In Chinatown, though, there had been big riots before the war and so the owners didn't want to take any risks. I can only remember a few fights between different ethnic groups. One night trouble broke out between the Malays and Chinese. It came to a head outside Sun Pictures with the Chinese wielding boat oars and the Malays fighting with broken bottles. We all ran for cover.

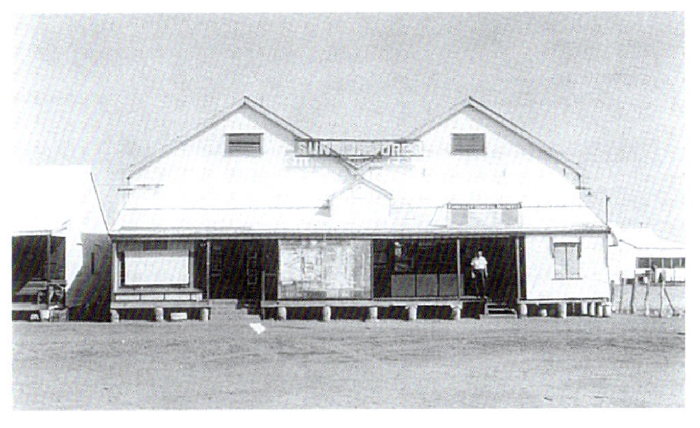

Sun Pictures, 1950s.

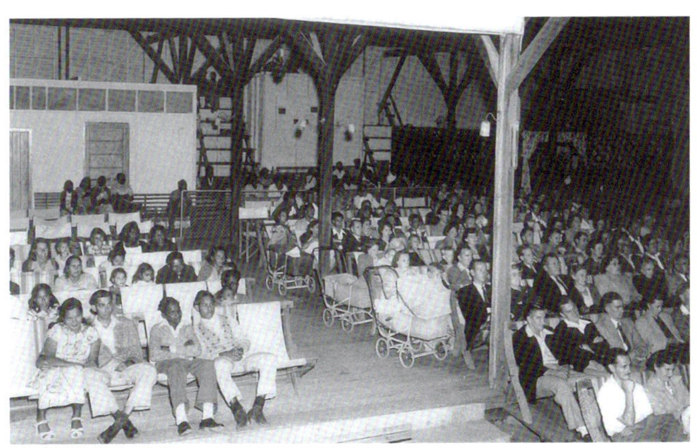

Inside at Sun Pictures — note the segregated seating where the Aboriginal people sat on the tiered seats at the back behind a fence. The coloured people were on the left and in the last few rows at the rear.

We often had to put up with discrimination against us from the European business-owners and this sometimes led to strikes. There were times when we coloureds refused to go into Sun Pictures. A strike could last for a couple of weeks and it might have started because someone was kicked out of his seat to give it to a white person. We wouldn't go back until the picture theatre boss had apologised to the leaders of the community.

Movies were on Tuesdays, Thursdays and Saturdays, but we rarely went weeknights because of school. Just about everybody went on Saturday night. Seating was segregated and then we were reminded who was who. Aboriginals were right at the back, fenced in, on wooden planks. Actually they had quite a good view of the screen on their tiered benches. The whites sat in the shaded area in the centre, and the sides were for the coloureds, which included Asians and mixed races. There were two exits and we would leave by the side door. When it was king tide, the water would be right around the cinema. The white men would lift up their wives and carry them so their dresses and shoes didn't get wet. The rest of us would have fun wading through the water.

The cowboy and Indian movies were hugely popular, and we would always cheer when the Indians got shot. To us the good guys were the cowboys and the bad boys were the Indians. Little did we realise that these were stories about the Indians fighting for their land. I loved 'Gone with the Wind', and I saw that movie at least three times. I think I related to it because they had racial categories like octoroon, mulatto and quadroons, and the story revealed the racial issues of America.

There was a big interval between movies, and we'd go over to the shops for treats. Where Wing's shop is now, there was a little Malay shop in a tin shed belonging to old man Yusuf. He had small tables made from planks from who-knows-where, and he'd put them on four-gallon kerosene tins. We'd sit around and have shaved-ice cordial and lollies. He had fowls in that room and they would get up on the tables while we were eating and drinking. When Yusuf closed down, Jan's squash shop opened up and we had lovely squash in big glasses with ice.

Anawei's original shop is where the Shekki Shed is today. He'd always be there in his blue and white striped boxers to serve us at any time of the day. The shop had shelves behind a huge timber counter, and he'd sleep on his counter when no one was there.

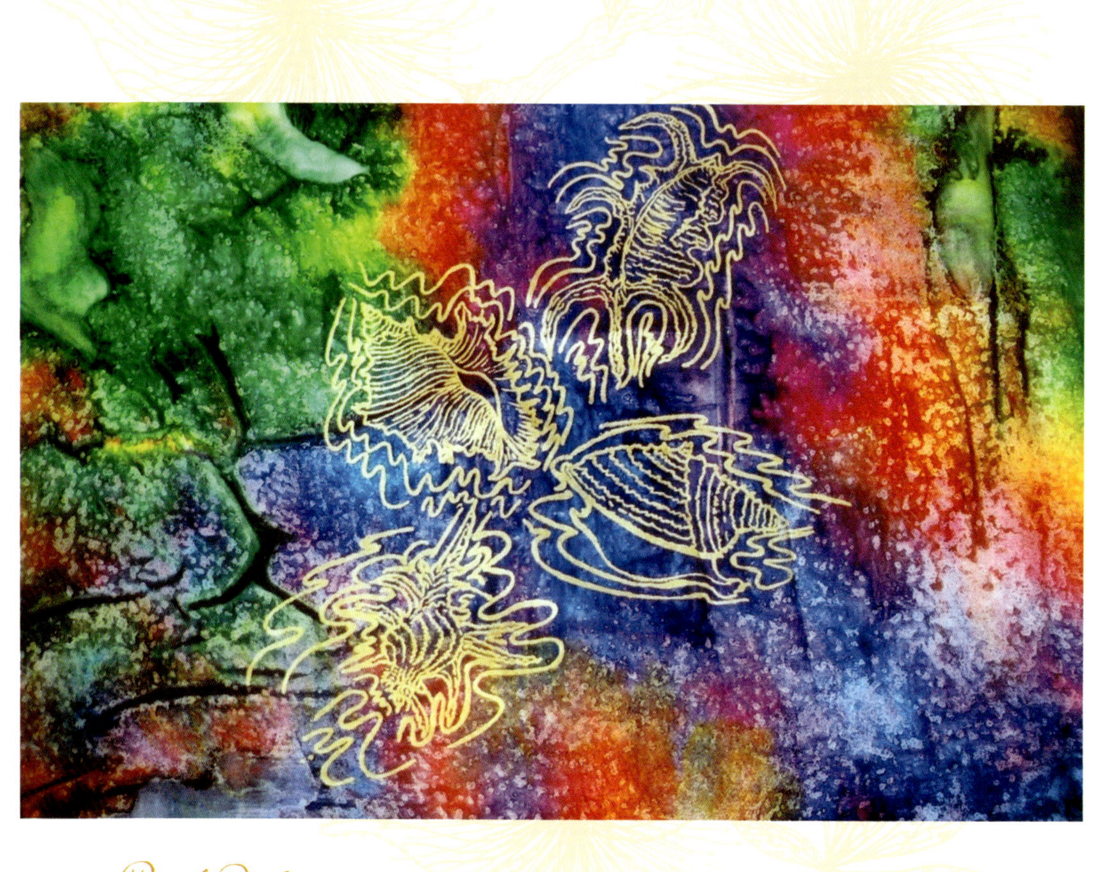

Rock Pool

The windows had iron bars and we'd sing out, 'Anawei! Anawei'. Sometimes he'd jump off the counter, still half-asleep, and we'd sing, 'Anawei, Anawei, don't go thataway, come here thisaway!' When he let us in, he'd serve us, then lock the door again and go back to sleep. Anawei sold chocolates and confectionary, and he made a killing on sticks of tobacco that he sold to the locals.

Next door was Ah Kim. Our parents would say, 'Don't buy satay from Ah Kim, he kills cats!' We'd get our money from them and the first thing we'd do was line up to get Ah Kim's satays. They were the softest meat. The cats would be sitting lined up on his roof. He had so many cats, but we ate the meat anyway. Hardly anyone went there except us kids.

John Chi Lane was where the Japanese shops were. This is not the same as the Johnny Chi Lane today — the name and its location have changed. My mother worked in John Chi's long soup shop before the war and knew the Japanese families well. It really was Chinatown in those days as there were hardly any European people. Now it is a proper gardiya place.

Chinatown smelt of the orient with exotic foods in every shop and home. The tempting aroma of Asian food filled the air and outside the pictures there would sometimes be satays and curries for sale. The Ellies' family owned a big store on the corner and you could always smell Singhalese cooking wafting down the street. Uncle Joe Torres made the best ice cream. He would ride in Chinatown on a little bike with his ice-cream cart in front, selling ice-cream in a cone. Because I was his niece, I never had to pay for mine.

The boarding houses were filled with Malays and Koepangers from Timor. You'd often see them upstairs on their verandahs playing ukuleles and mandolins, and singing traditional songs from home.

Many of the different ethnic groups had their own clubs. Both the Japanese club and the Filipino club shut down during the war and never reopened, but the Indonesian–Malay club held an important place in our lives. We went there on many Friday nights for parties with our families. There were big suppers, dancing and everybody had a wonderful time.

That was where we first saw the popular dances of the day, including the cha cha, rumba, samba, foxtrot, waltze and the jitterbug. The Malays and the Indonesians were renowned for their cha cha, rumba and samba, whereas the local boys like Alf Corpus, Eddie Roe and Jack Lee were great dancers of the waltz, foxtrot and

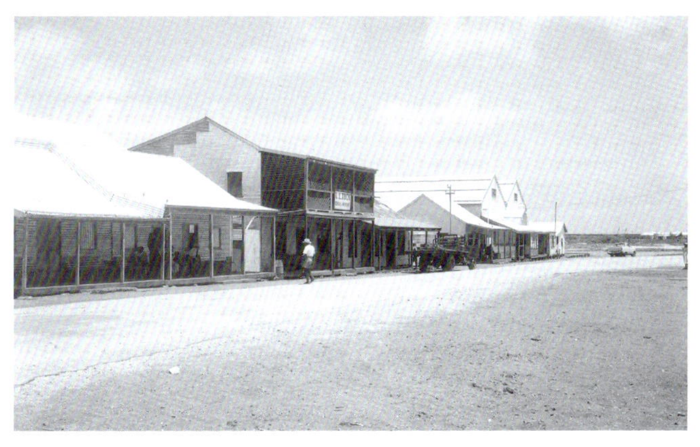

Carnarvon Street in the late 1950s.
Ltor: Anawei's, Tack's and Wing's.
Sun Pictures is at the end with the peaked roof.

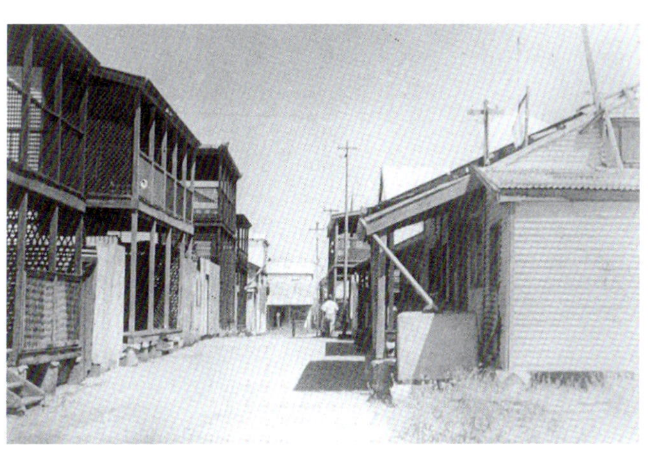

Shiba Lane, before the war.

the jitterbug. One of the Malay men, though, was also renowned for the jitterbug. Some people still talk about 'Jitterbug Johnny' today.

The older girls, like Margie Roe and her sister, Tanni, and Hasma and Una Rahman were also terrific dancers and we loved to watch them. Today, whenever I hear the big band sound of Glenn Miller's 'In the Mood' and 'Moonlight Serenade', it takes me back to those carefree days and I can imagine Aunty Biddy and Uncle Salem gliding across the floor.

Many of the European women from Melbourne, who had married Asian men, would be at the club with their husbands. They were really friendly to us, and I was fascinated by their clothes and their bright-red lipstick. I'd love to get a kiss from one of them and rub the lipstick on my cheeks like rouge. We were used to pearling master's wives who just let us be, and government official's wives who were inclined to put on airs and graces. The Melbourne women were the first white women, other than the nuns, to open up their arms to us, and they brought in another type of culture from the city. It must have been very hard for them leaving Melbourne and finding their place in Broome society. They had stepped outside 'accepted' social behaviour so they couldn't mix with the other Europeans. However, in Broome, they became part of our families and community.

After the war Shiba Lane was still there, but the renowned brothels were bolted. There were empty houses too, along the lane where people squatted. People stayed anywhere. A few of my aunties lived along Shiba Lane and we used to play around that area. Although our aunties warned us not to peek into the abandoned brothels, the first thing we would do was find the biggest crack and look through. Up on the walls, there'd be framed pictures of glamorous Japanese women, revealing legs and shoulders in seductive poses. Oh, you never saw women's legs and shoulders so bare! Apart from those Japanese men who had married Aboriginal women and who returned to Broome years later, there were no Japanese left. They had all been sent home.

There were only a few Asian shops and restaurants remaining in Chinatown — Tang Wei's, Yusuf's, Anawei's, Ah Kim's, Fong Sam's, Tack's, Ah Ming's, Dep's, Ellies' — although there were still Indonesians, Malays and a few old Filipinos living around the area. We used to live for the taste of Tang Wei's long soup. It was *the* restaurant in town and his long soup was famous.

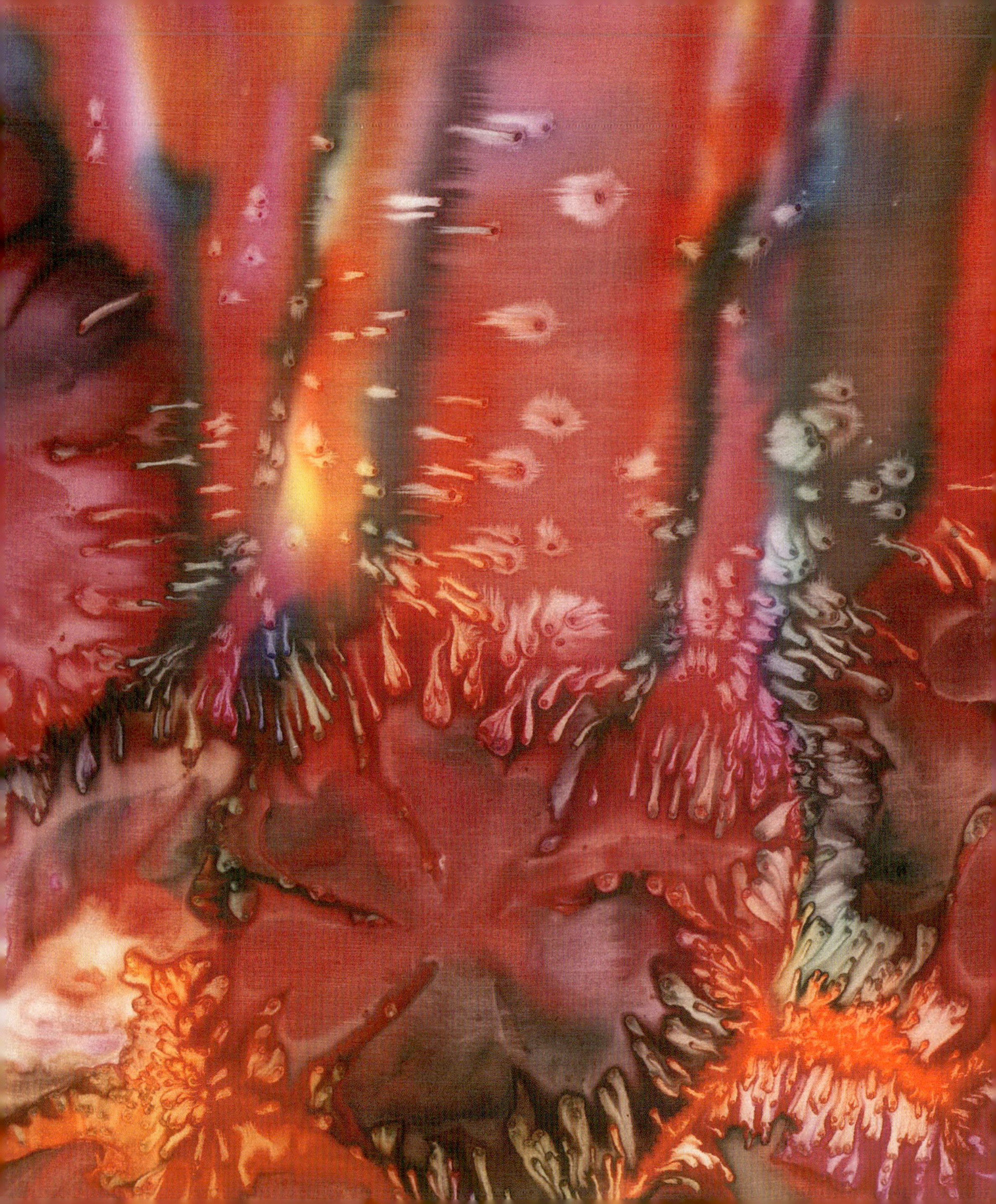

The Luggers

After the war, Broome slowly rebuilt itself. There was still demand for pearl shell, but it didn't last. The market had been too drastically affected by the replacement of pearl shell buttons with plastic varieties. It wasn't until the mid-1950s that the first pearls began to be cultivated on pearl farms around the Kimberley coast.

The only boats in those immediate post-war days were still the pearling luggers and their dinghies. Sometimes the local Aboriginals would borrow the dinghies to get dugong and turtles.

Although the luggers would never return to their pre-war numbers of around four hundred, those that remained looked beautiful when they came in at full sail, silhouetted against the soft colours of Roebuck Bay at sunrise and sunset. On balmy nights when we were eating outside, we'd hear the chug of the engines as the luggers headed into Broome. One lugger would come in, then another, then a couple more.

We spent most of our childhood days with women because the men would often be away for weeks at a time working on the luggers. Diving was a dangerous job for little money, and there were many deaths. Sometimes a diver's air-line got tangled or cut, or for some reason he would come to the surface too quickly and get the 'bends'. Each diver never knew if it was going to be his last trip.

I remember that in 1956 there were several deaths. One time a diver's air was shut off accidentally from his air-line. Another diver's helmet came off under water because it hadn't been screwed on tightly enough. One diver's air-line got caught around the propeller of the boat.

On those days people would be fishing on the jetty and would come running in, shouting, 'Lugger coming, half-mast!' That meant a death. The other luggers that were working in the same area where the death had occurred, even if they were from another company, came in behind it to show respect.

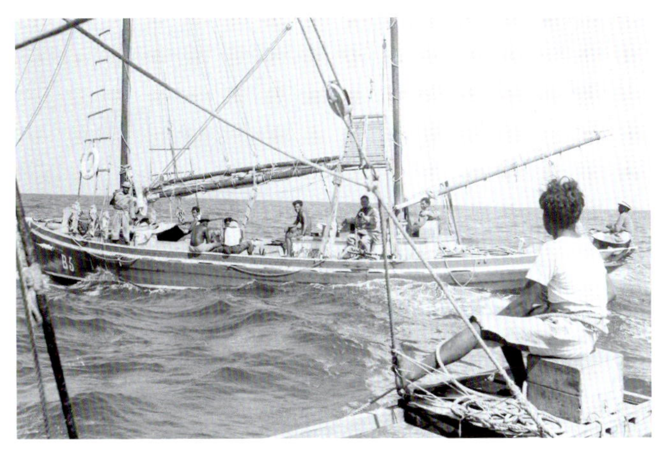

Divers take a rest on their lugger, while the tender in the foreground has his diver at work, 1949.

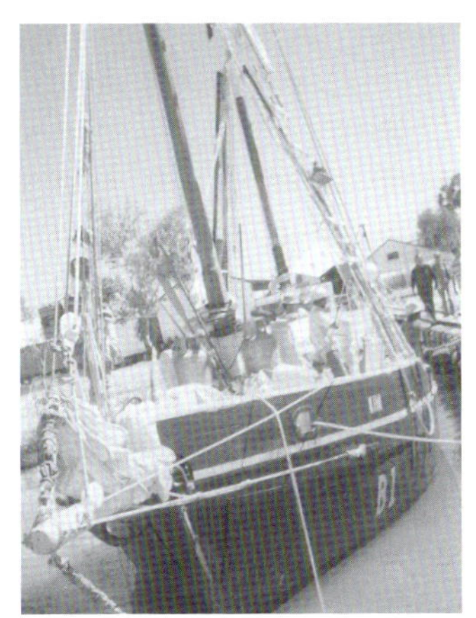

Streeter's Jetty, 1950s.

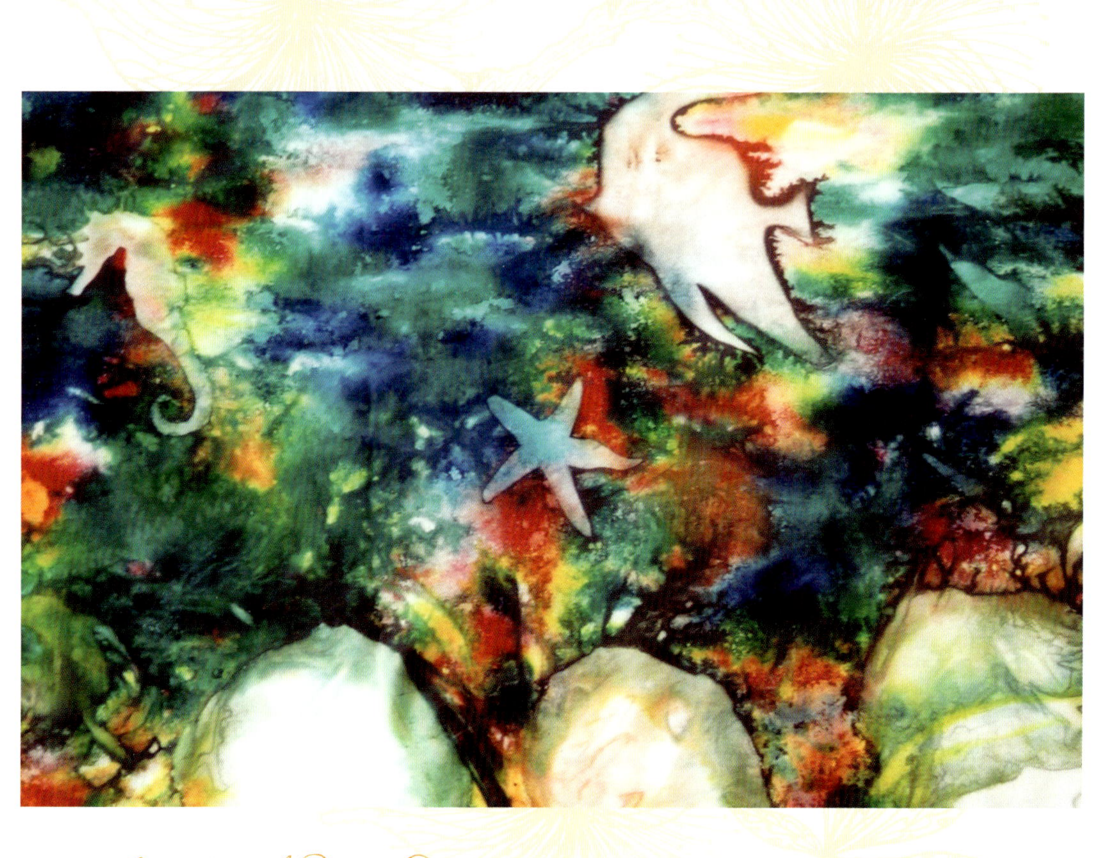

Mother of Pearl Dreaming

The pearling masters would look through their binoculars and identify which lugger was on its way. The wives didn't know who had died until the boats got to shore, as there were two divers on each boat. Workers' compensation wasn't heard of then and although some of the pearling masters looked after the workers' families, many had to fend for themselves. Sam Male is still remembered and respected by Broome families for the way he looked after the families of his divers. He provided employment for the coloureds and Aboriginals in his shops, and in many areas of his business. Local people worked as shell packers, boat builders, sail makers and as crew on the luggers.

One great celebration was the lugger picnic. The picnic was held each year on the weekend before the beginning of a new season. Lay-up was from December to late February during cyclone season, and was the time for repairing the boats. To mark the new season, the lugger crews invited everyone in town to the picnic, kids and all. It was believed that you increased your luck by the amount of people you had on your lugger, meaning less chance of deaths on the lugger and more chance of finding shell. If you were to find a natural

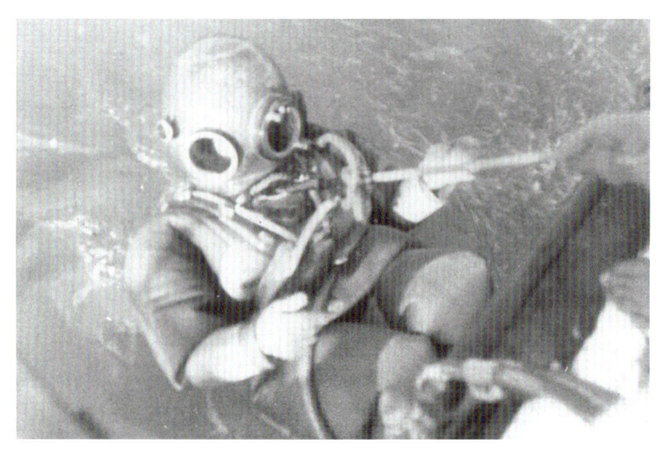

Diver in 'full dress', 1950s.

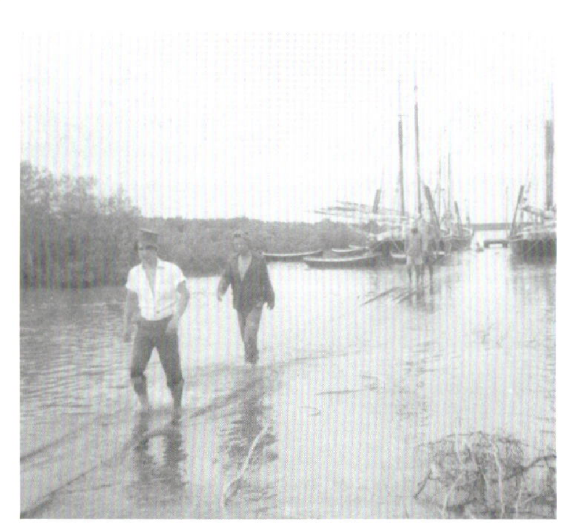

Lugger crew coming in from Streeter's Jetty.

pearl, that would be a bonus. We had a ball, hopping from boat to boat where we were welcomed to boost up the numbers. There was always enough food and drink to last a week. Everyone got merry, and the parties would go on for days.

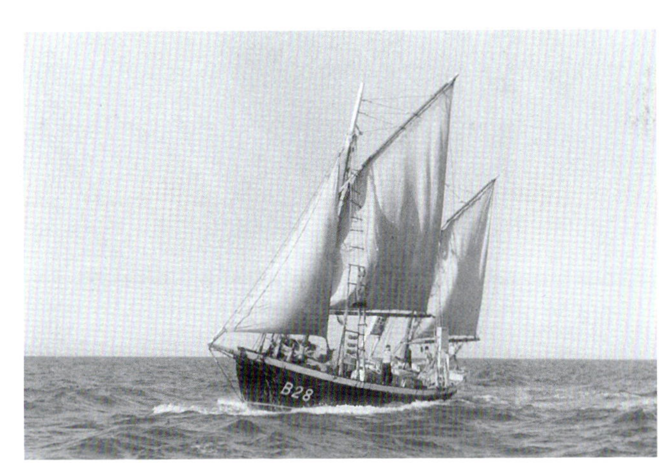

A lugger in full sail out on Roebuck Bay, 1950s.

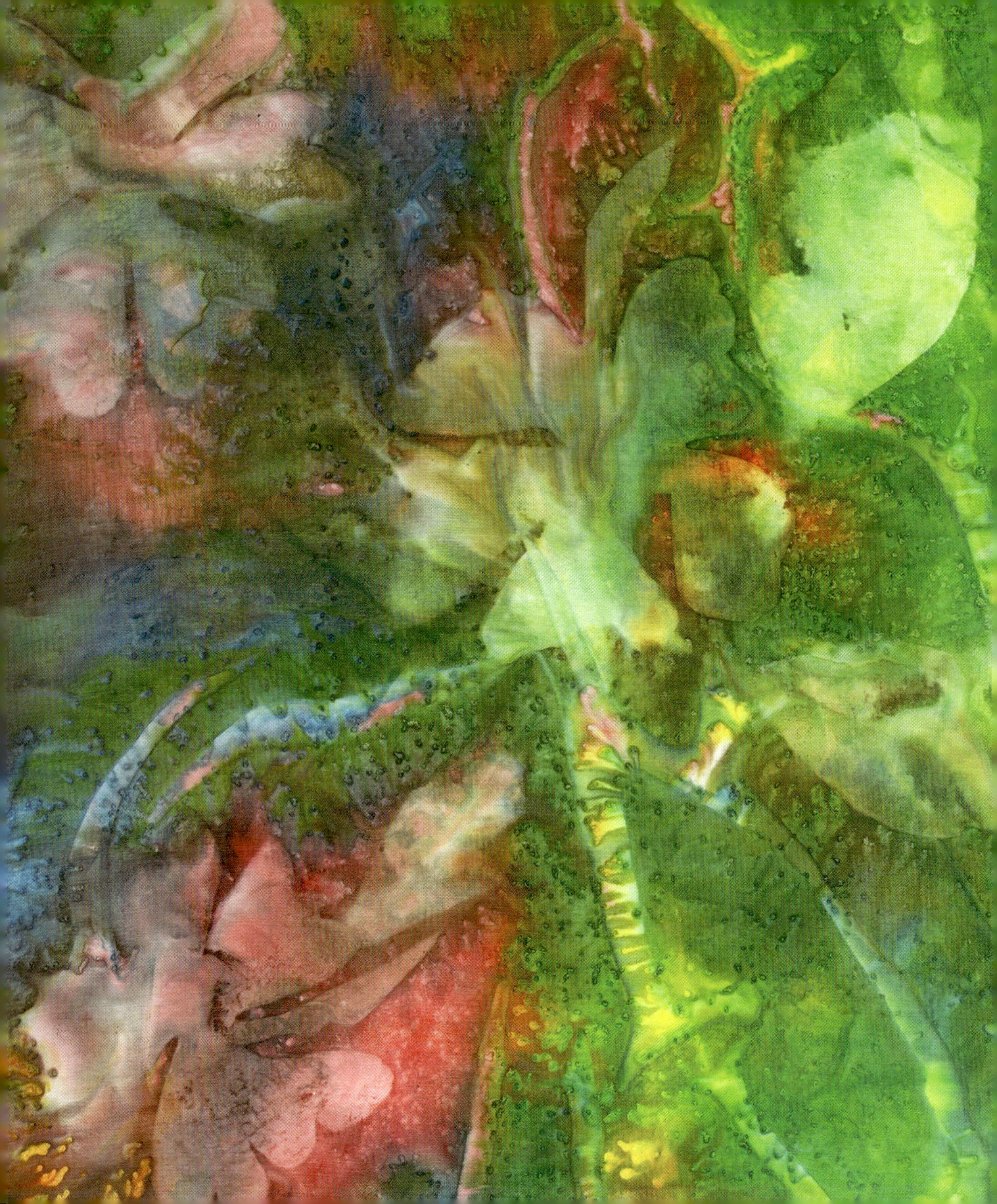

Celebrations

Most of the nuns in the St John of God convent were Irish, and St Patrick's Day was a huge feast day. At St Mary's every child had to have something green on — green ribbons, green dresses, green socks. If you didn't, you had to find a leaf to pin on. We'd have a party with games and dancing, and then we would have the afternoon free.

Many of our church activities were also influenced by Filipino and Indonesian Catholic traditions. For our Easter festivities, we would start a week before, on Palm Sunday. Like the Filipinos and Indonesians, we prepared for Palm Sunday by plaiting palms in different patterns. We would then carry them in a procession around the churchyard. Wednesday night was the mass for the blessing of the oils, Thursday was the mass for the Last Supper, Friday was Stations of the Cross, and Saturday was Easter Vigil. On Easter Sunday we went to High Mass with all the priests.

In May, it was our school feast day. We performed the Filipino custom of the ceremonial 'Crowning of Our Lady', and a boy and a girl would be chosen to carry the crown. They would both be dressed in white, with the girl wearing a veil. The statue of Mary would be up on a bench, and the boy had the job of putting a small stool there and helping the girl reach up and crown Our Lady. For weeks we would be on our best behaviour hoping to be chosen. I desperately wanted to be picked, but I was always disappointed and believed that I must have been too naughty. When I look back today, I suspect it had more to do with the situation at home. Simeon was Muslim and living with my mother, and I was illegitimate. Although this was more accepted in the wider community, the church laws reflected a much stricter view.

First Holy Communion was celebrated on the Feast of Christ the King, in October. That was another big event. We thought we had to be pure for the whole year, and we did our best not to swear, especially in the month before. When we made our first communion we were like brides in our white clothes, silks, taffetas, and organzas. Our veils were made from mosquito netting with flowers and bows, and we thought we were beautiful! I remember when my cousin, Maureen Howard, had to take her communion and her father had just died. Everybody worked together to make sure she had everything. She was dressed beautifully.

I was about eight when I made my First Communion, and I was very excited about the communion breakfast held at the convent. The sisters set out the food on long tables under the mango trees, with cloths and flowers, and we invited our family and friends.

It was, however, hard to be pure for long. Straight after our communion breakfast and after having been so good for months, the first thing my friend, Mary-Rose Lee, and I did was take mangoes from Mrs McDaniel's tree. She lived opposite the convent and the mangoes were hanging down over the fence, temptingly ripe, ready to be picked and eaten. We helped ourselves, and I remember the old postmaster's wife observing us from across the road.

Red-faced and screaming, she yelled, 'Stealing from an old woman, you naughty, naughty girls!'

I was Confirmed when I was twelve. Incense permeated the

air and the church was decorated with candles and flowers. Again we wore white, girls on one side of the aisle and boys on the other. Confirmation was always held in the evening and the long mass was said in Latin. I suspect I dozed off.

On the church calendar, there are many Holy Days of Obligation. All Saints' Day is on the first of November and so we didn't have school. The day before All Saints' Day we were reminded of who we'd been named after, and we would have to tell the other children about that saint's life and his or her saintly qualities. I had been named after St Ursula, as well as my godmother.

All Souls' Day is the following day and is set aside to remember our loved ones who had died. Children weren't allowed to go to funerals but we were allowed to go to the Novena, the nine nights of Rosary which began on the day of the burial. I believe this custom was introduced by the Filipinos, and it is still a big part of the mourning ritual in Broome today.

An important Muslim religious celebration was the Malay celebration of Hari Raya Aidilfitri, which marked the end of the fasting month of Ramadhan. It was a time of praying for those who had passed away, and a time of sharing within the Muslim community.

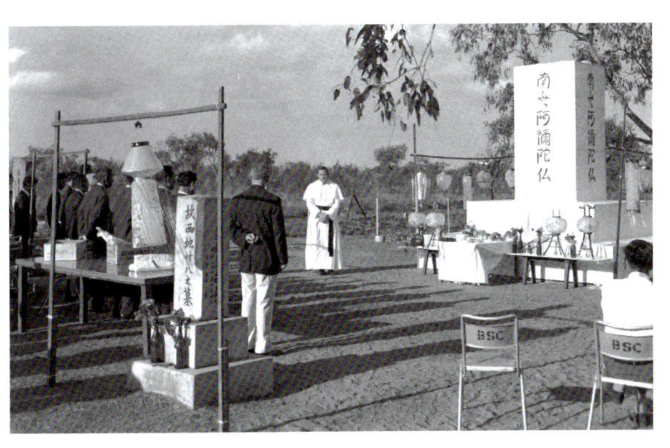

Japanese ceremony, Broome cemetery, late 1950s.

Anzac Day was also significant. As it wasn't long after the war, it really meant something. We'd get up at five in the morning, and a boy and a girl were chosen to lay the wreath at the war memorial in Bedford Park. It was always exciting to hear the guns and the canon go off.

August was a special month because it was the time when all the ethnic groups held festivals. There was a ten-day break and the luggers would come into town. The Japanese celebrated their 'Bon' festival during the August Moon, and the Chinese celebrated 'Hang Seng' (Hung Ting). These were their feasts for the dead and they were held a day apart. Indonesians, Malaysians and Singaporeans also

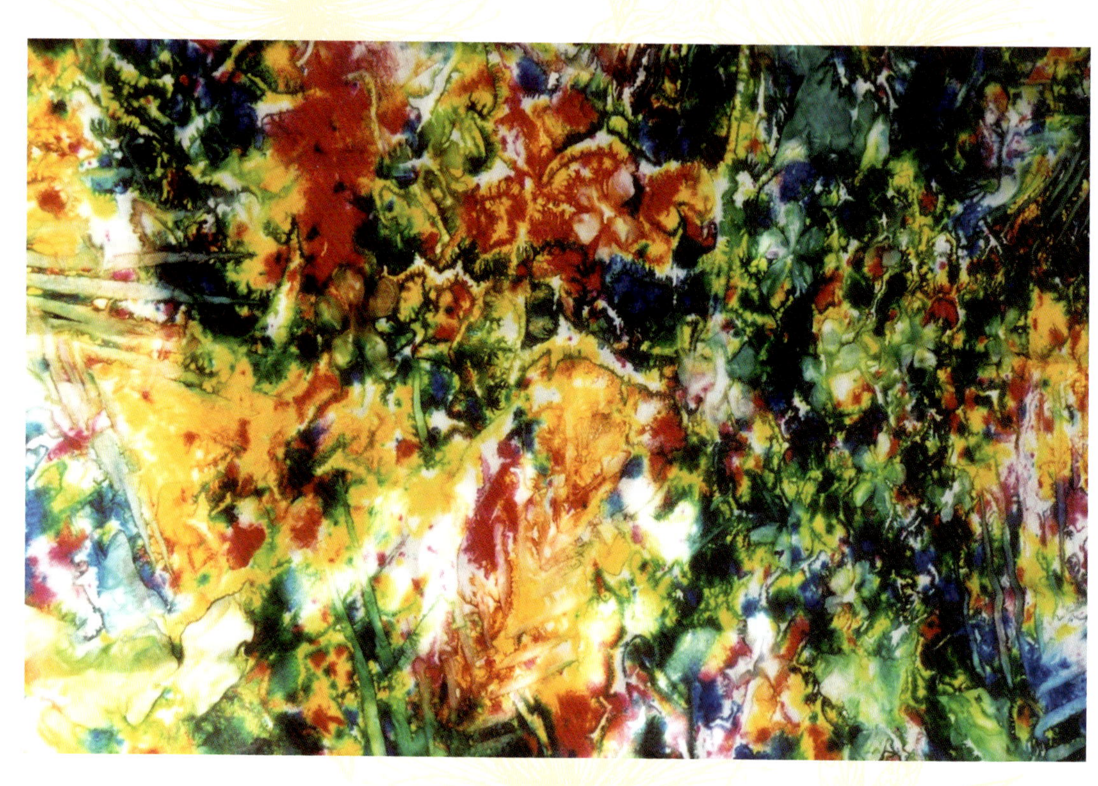

Tropical Bloom 1

celebrated their 'Merdeka' (Independence Day) at that time. The origins of 'Shinju Matsuri', the annual 'Festival of the Pearl' which was first held in Broome in 1969, lie in these traditional festivals.

Guy Fawkes Night was always a big event. We couldn't wait to get our crackers from Chinatown. The Chinese shops brought in a great range from Singapore and Hong Kong, and children would save their pennies for months ahead. We would have a big night at someone's house, and let off our crackers. There were skyrockets, jumping jacks, little red Chinese crackers in all sizes, from tiny ones to huge big bombs. We'd call the red ones 'penny bungers' and the boys would throw them under the house to scare the old people. It's a wonder the houses didn't burn down! There were beautiful golden showers, which were stuck in the ground and would spray like a waterfall, and of course, there were sparklers. We'd use ours up and then look across to Chinatown where a big show would be going on. The shopkeepers' kids were the rich kids and so we'd sit back and watch.

There was this poor old white derelict called Lofty, who lived among us, and he could see what was happening. One year he decided to play 'Robin Hood', and he robbed bags of fireworks off the Chinese shopkeepers. We had fireworks for over a week and let them off at every house. We were still going when Chinatown was in darkness. The shopkeepers had none left because Lofty had given them to us.

Linju (police) came, took him away and I think he got six months. He robbed the Chinese shops to keep the kids happy. Lofty was also what they called a 'supplier'. He'd go into the pub, buy alcohol for anyone without a permit, and then take a tip to earn his living. If suppliers got caught they usually did six months in gaol. Poor Lofty was punished, but it was the best Guy Fawkes Night we ever had.

In December it was Christmas, and the most special of all our celebrations. For weeks before, Mum would get catalogues sent up from Perth so that she could order our presents. We made our own decorations from crepe paper, and streamers, bells and balloons would be strung up all over people's verandahs. Pearl and I would get down on our hands and knees and would scrub and polish our verandah to make sure everything looked perfect. Our Christmas tree was usually a wattle tree from the bush.

Mum would always reinforce the significance of Christmas and we weren't allowed to celebrate it unless we had been to mass. Midnight mass was our favourite because it was always packed, and we usually got a new dress for the occasion. We had to walk to church and, depending on where we were living at the time, it could be quite a long walk. If it was raining we missed out, and we would have to go to mass on Christmas Day.

After midnight mass the young men would jump on the back of utes and drive around town, visiting homes, singing Christmas carols, and playing their guitars, mandolins and ukuleles. Their songs continued throughout the night and into Christmas and Boxing Day. Sometimes the party would continue until New Year. This celebration would involve the whole community, and each family would provide drinks and food.

Bathing Shed Beach was our favourite spot to celebrate birthdays, and we'd often go there for someone's twenty-first. Whole families would attend and it would usually turn into a moonlight beach party. Everybody would bring food and the adults would gather around the fire, singing and dancing the night away.

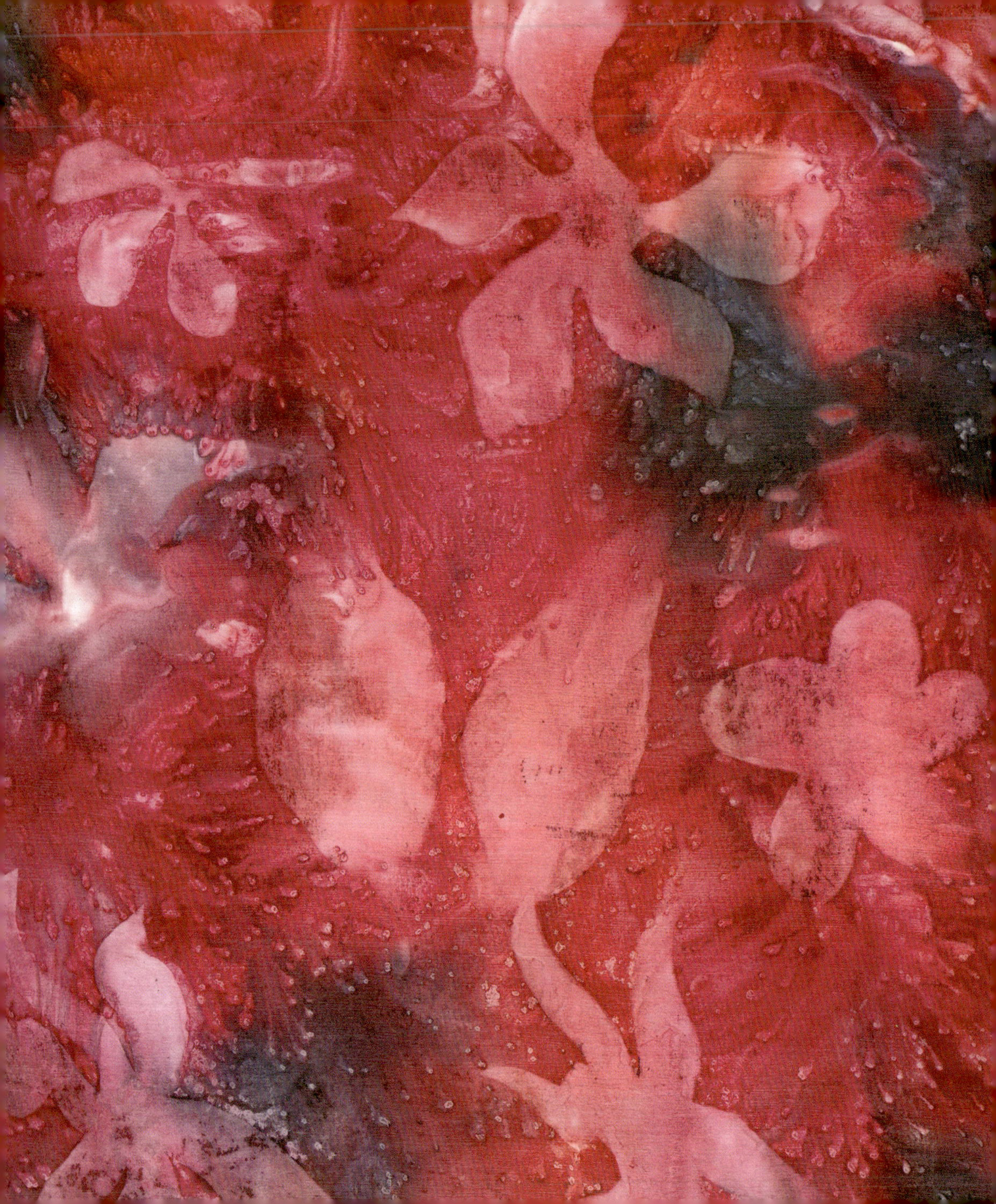

Seasons

As the cycle of the seasons turned, plans would be made for trips down to the ocean or into the bush to collect whatever nature could provide. *Mayi* (bush food) was not only tasty to eat, but lots of fun to get. We would dig up bush potatoes and onions, and collect any fruit that we knew was ready to eat.

From early January to March, during the rainy season, Broome became abundant with bush fruits. The rainy season was cyclone time. 'Rainy season soon, rainy season coming.' We didn't call it the 'wet'. In the season we went for *gubinge*. We used to love our gubinge. Some are nice, sweet and juicy, and some so sour they make your eyes water. They're green and round with a little point, and the size of a thumbnail. The white ones are the sweetest. The sap from the tree is delicious too, and we would either eat it straight like toffee or take it home and boil it in water and sugar to soften it.

The bush fruit *gamolon* was also in the same season. As they got riper, they would get whiter and almost translucent. That was another taste again, but we loved it. Now, I can't even get my grandchildren to taste it. Once upon a time we would walk for miles, right out to Cable Beach, to get it.

Guwal, the white fruit-like clumps of grapes as tiny as rice, were my favourite around Christmas, but my favourite bush food was *gungkara*. They are like blackberries. They used to be in the bushland behind Herbert Street, but sadly, there aren't many trees now. The middle of the year was gungkara season, and we'd be out after school collecting them. We had to be home by five because we weren't allowed in the bush after dark. It would be cold and we'd have jumpers on. We'd fill enamel pannikins to take home for mum, but sometimes there weren't many left by the time we got there! Gubinge, guwal and gamolan all grew on the coast near the sand dunes, whereas gungkara could be found closer to town.

Magabala was never one of my favourite fruits as I found it too dry. Some people call it the 'bush banana', and others know it as the 'bush cucumber'.

Many of the wonderful old trees around Broome have now gone, but when I was a girl there used to be a big *mangarr* tree outside the hospital, where the carpark is now. The ripe fruit of the mangarr was dark blue and it was very sweet. There were many sandalwood trees too, with a delicious fruit similar to a blackberry.

The town was dotted with boab trees and we'd climb up and get the nuts. Some would be pretty wet when we cracked them open, and we'd eat them half-green, before they got too dry. There are many shapes and sizes of nuts, and they all taste different. There was also the fruit we knew as 'Taylor fruit', and we'd walk for miles to the only tree at One Mile to eat it. Tamarind was another favourite, and we'd climb up to the highest branches to eat the fruit, especially the boys who would race each other to the top.

Old man Chukani lived where Frederick Street ended, at the rubbish tip, and that was another place we went looking for fruit, especially watermelons and pig melons. Old man Chukani would save us the big watermelons, and have them lined up when we got there after school. They were always lying close to where they emptied the toilet pans. There was an old dump close by where they buried the sewage, and it was old man Chukani's job to clean the pans. Two days a week the sanitation truck would come around the town and we'd be yelling, 'Shit truck coming! Who's in toilet? Get out of toilet, shit truck coming!'

The Camps

It is hard to believe that a fence ran down Herbert Street right through town and the full-bloods had to live outside of the fenced area. We loved to go into the bush where they lived because there was so much bush fruit, and it didn't seem to matter how hot it was. One time I remember my cousin, Irene Shiosaki, had a bleeding nose after walking in the burning heat.

When we were out searching, we would come upon the bush camps and would stop and talk with the old people. They would always give us water, so sometimes we'd say, 'Let's go to camp and get a drink.' Of course, like most children, we lived for the moment and didn't think about using up their water supply.

The bush was full of kangaroo traps. We'd see the fruit and

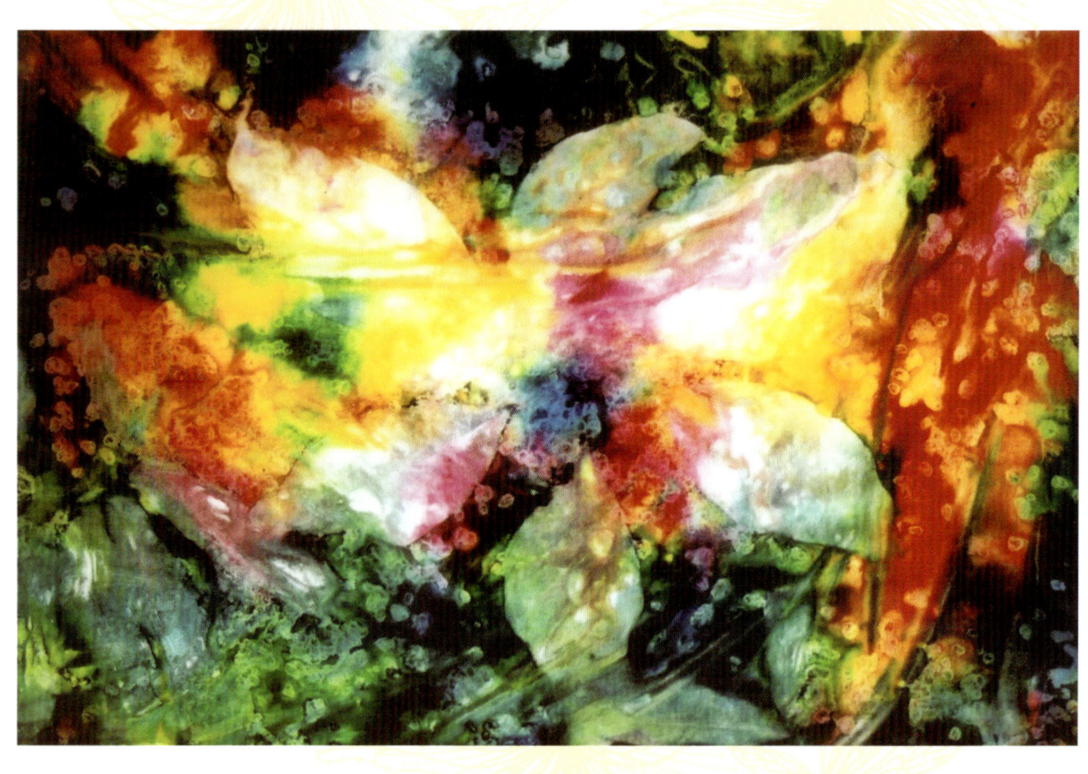

Wet Season Dreaming

go running flat out towards it, but then we would see a wire loop tied onto the tree just in time, and screech to a halt. Kangaroos would hop near the tree and get their leg caught in the ring of wire. I used to like a yummy kangaroo-tail stew. I remember eating it in Beagle Bay but I haven't had it since then.

For the old people that lived near Herbert and Barker Streets, that place was like a sacred area, and the bush camps were spotless. Many had been living in the missions before they came to Broome. They were still traditional, but they wore western clothes.

As well as drinking their water, we also ate half their food. They'd be sitting around the fire cooking damper, and we'd hang around and share their tucker. We'd mainly go talk to a distinguished old man by the name of Sebastian. He was very tall and strong and had a grey beard. He'd feed the *loongoord* (blue tongue lizards) to keep the snakes out.

Their shelters were bough sheds with four posts and thatched roofs made from branches. Outside was their cooking area. They'd have big tidy yards with no leaves, and the old women raked and weeded because they couldn't stand double gees (prickles). They didn't wear shoes and hated treading on prickly plants, introduced by the Europeans when they brought in their sheep and cattle. They would make their own brooms and sweep the camps clean. If one leaf floated down it would be burnt in the campfire. I don't know where the old people went when it rained and at willy-willy time.

If we were going out to the bush camps, our parents would warn us to be careful and not touch anything we saw under the trees such as a boomerang, string or cloth. It was sacred ground and these items would be used for their kabakabas.

We went to a few kabakabas and they were very exciting. At certain parts of the kabakaba, women had to keep their heads down because it was men's business. I am not sure what went on. We were so scared when we were told not to look that I never took a peek. The men were always painted up with ochre. They wore ornamental pearl shells, and carried spears and boomerangs. Even when we didn't go, we'd hear them chanting during the night. When the authorities moved all the people from Herbert Street out to One Mile, we still went out there for the kabakabas.

Superstitions

We all grew up to be superstitious. Malays and Indonesians are very strong about black magic as well as many Aboriginal people.

We were terrified of *goomboons*. They were big, hairy, monster women with huge *nyanyas* (breasts), and our parents always warned us about them. The goomboon was similar to a yeti and lived in the mangroves. It was drummed into us that if a goomboon captured one of us, we would be picked up, tucked under the weight of a goomboon nyanya, and grown up in the mangroves never to see our mothers again. Needless to say, this ensured that we were home safely before dark.

There were also the 'little people'. Our parents said that the little people would come and take us if we were out after dark. We believed that they lived on Cable Beach, and we always made sure that we were home on time. There were also the little men who lived in the cork trees in town. We knew them as 'kofris', and it is only now that I think that they were probably the same little people that lived out at Cable Beach.

Weld Street was one of the haunted streets where all the ghosts would come out at night. The 'Fiery-tongued Dog' lived in the block between Weld, Hamersley and Robinson Streets. It was the scariest place in Broome. A lot of people have seen it. Myself, Pearl, Betty Hassan and the Matsumoto family were coming back from netball one night when we heard a woman scream. It was an agonising and horrific scream.

We took off, and the woman yelled after us, 'Wait for me! Wait for me!'

We stopped to wait for her under a streetlight, but by the time she got to us she was pale and weak, and unable to speak properly. The Fiery-tongued Dog had leapt out at her.

Another ghost that used to scare people was the 'woman in white'. She had long flowing hair, and floated around that same area. She would turn her head to look right into people's souls with her piercing eyes, and she still wanders the streets today.

One of my greatest fears were lizards. I was terrified of *barndily*. We called them 'spitty barndily' because of their habit of ejecting fluid from under their tail when under threat. You don't see them much around anymore, and our parents would tell us to watch out for them. Their warnings made these small lizards seem very dangerous. We were also constantly being warned about snakes. They were everywhere, and some would make a kind of low mooing sound, I suppose when they were mating.

'Listen *banunburu* (python) is singing,' my mother would say.

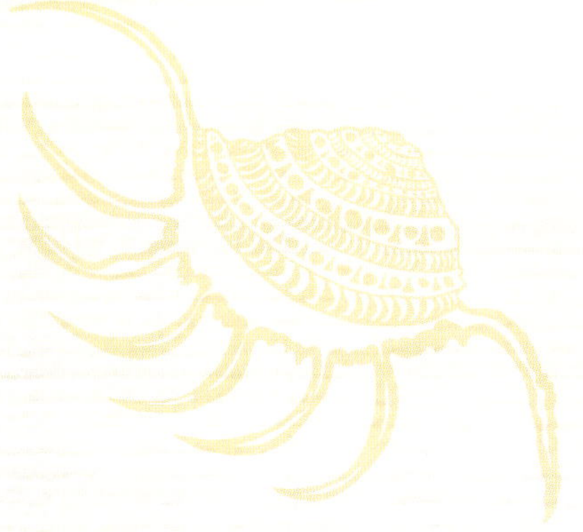

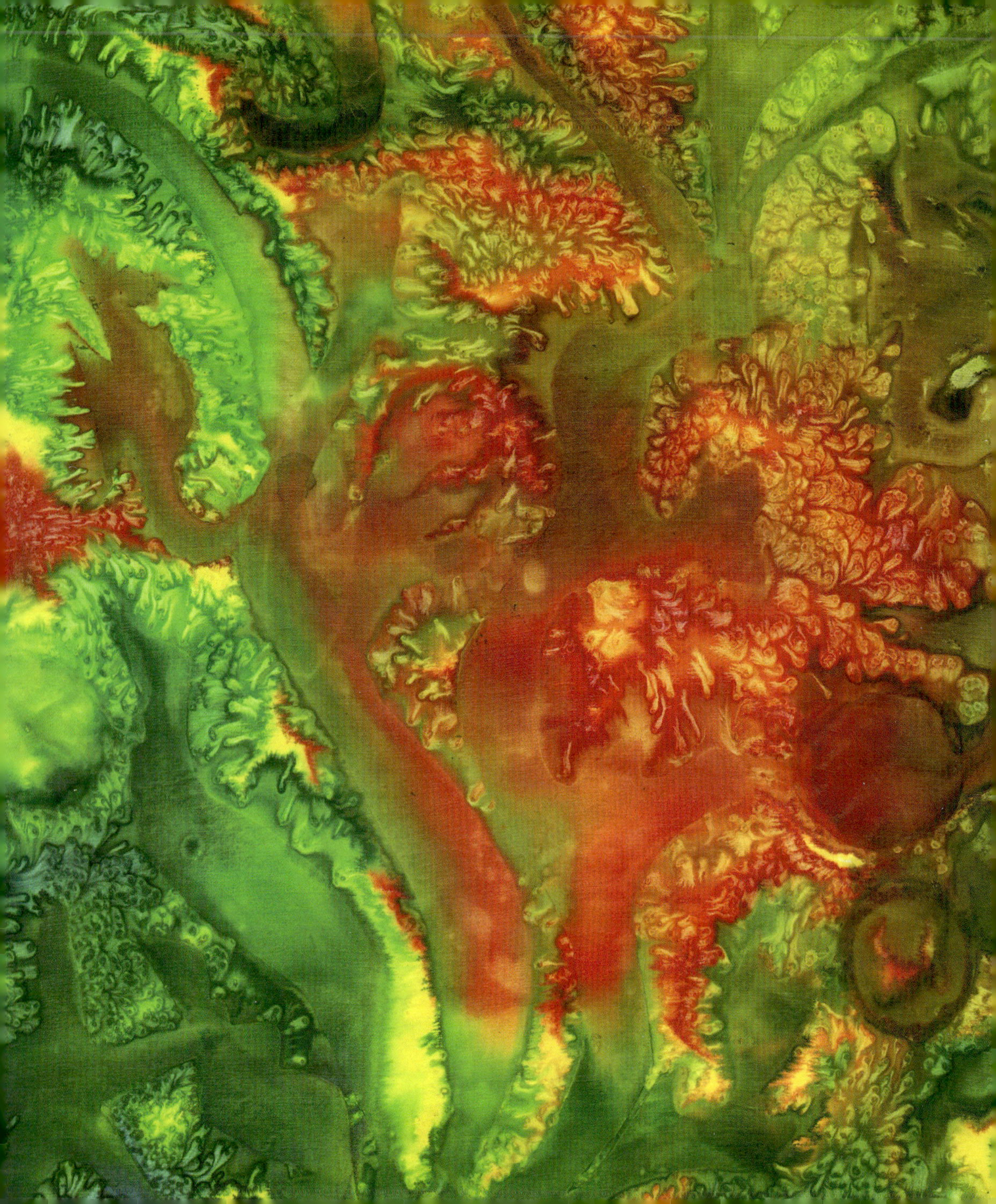

Gambling

In the heyday of the pearling years, Broome was famous for its gambling. Although there was still a gambling house when I was growing up, gambling mostly took place in people's houses. *Katjakatja* (similar to dominoes but with numbered brickettes) and *salang* (card games) were the drawcards when the luggers came in.

People would say, 'Eee, tonight we got big game *katjakatja* at so-and-so's place!' *Katjakatja* was a Broome word for *kachau kachau*, a Malay word meaning 'to stir' or 'mix it up', and was the local term for the Chinese game known as 'Bacau'. In Broome, the game evolved to include a mix of Japanese, Malay and Chinese words with Broome English and all the locals understood it. It's just like Stephen Pigram's song 'Feel Like Going Back Home' from *Bran Nue Dae*, the

Aboriginal musical by Jimmy Chi and the Broome band, 'Kuckles'. One verse in the song describes it well:

The luggers are in on the spring tide
The gambling house is packed
Banker he makan (eat) with siton (king card)
But larri (run) we got buttah (dead card) in front.

Mr Dep owned several boarding houses and the only licensed gambling house in town. The gambling house was mainly patronised by the Asian and coloured men — women were strictly forbidden entry. The stakes, however, were so lucrative that some of the more determined local women would dress up as men, and wear hats, baggy shirts and pants to gain entry. Aboriginal people were only allowed in if they held citizenship papers. There were times when Mr Dep's clientele would prefer to gamble with the women at home and then the police would get tipped off. Raids were common and, on one particular occasion, when a house on the marsh got raided, the gamblers were frog-marched to the police station carrying the tables, with the cards and money still lying on top.

When I was a child the big game was *cheefah*. It was a Chinese game, like a raffle, and was conducted in Chinese with the characters printed onto tickets. There were no Roman numerals to help you understand. It didn't matter what language you spoke, everyone knew how to read a cheefah ticket!

The banker would choose which character was the winner, and he would then give a *mundei* (riddle). Cheefah men sold the tickets, and they would tell people the mundei to help them make their selection. The mundei might be something like 'jump jump in saucepan', which would be number twenty-five or twenty-seven. Sometimes the meanings were quite rude. Each number represented a symbol of sorts and we would choose which one.

'Anyone *pasang* (bet)? Anyone got *kintot* (omen)?', the cheefah men would call out as they walked past our house.

'Did you dream anything significant?'

Believe it or not, even we bought our own tickets. If I dreamt of dogs then there was a chance that it would come out in cheefah, and the money would go on 'dog' and its pair, 'rat'. It was like two sides of a coin — heads and tails. All the characters and numbers on the ticket had a symbolic meaning, and when the cheefah man

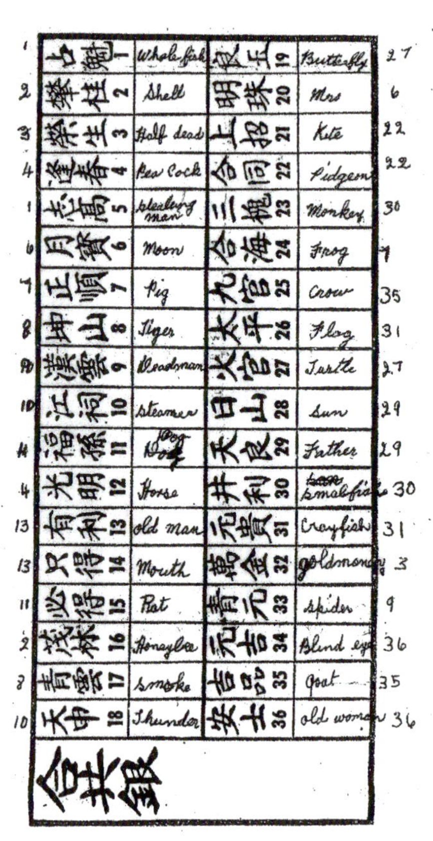

1	占魁 1	Whole fish	良玉 19	Butterfly	27
2	扳桂 2	Shell	明珠 20	Mrs	6
3	榮生 3	Half dead	上招 21	Kite	22
4	逢春 4	Pea Cock	合同 22	Pidgeon	22
1	志高 5	Stealing man	三槐 23	Monkey	30
6	月寶 6	Moon	合海 24	Frog	7
7	正順 7	Pig	九官 25	Crow	35
8	坤山 8	Tiger	太平 26	Flag	31
9	漢雲 9	Deadman	火官 27	Turtle	27
10	江祠 10	Steamer	日山 28	Sun	29
11	福孫 11	~~Dog~~ Dog	天良 29	Father	29
4	光明 12	Horse	井利 30	~~Lean~~ smalfish	30
13	有利 13	old man	元貴 31	Crayfish	31
13	只得 14	Mouth	萬金 32	goldmoney	3
11	必得 15	Rat	青元 33	Spider	9
2	茂林 16	Honeybee	元吉 34	Blind eye	36
8	青雲 17	smoke	吉品 35	Goat	35
10	天申 18	Thunder	安士 36	old woman	36

合共銀

A cheefah ticket.

came to collect bets, you would look for signs. You would bet on whatever symbol held meaning for you, and place money on the first symbol with some on the behind. A similar comparison would be the modern-day win-and-place betting system.

If you dreamt about someone dying, you bet on number thirty-two, 'half dead', and 'gold money' behind. 'Gold money' also symbolised a snake, so if you dreamt of a snake or saw one that day, your money would go on gold money.

If someone stole something from you, you bet on number one, 'whale fish', and number three, 'stealing man' behind. If anything fell down, or things made a loud noise, it was *guru guru*, thunder.

'Oh, good *kintot*. It's raining!' we'd say and put three shillings on guru guru and one on 'steamer' behind.

'Butterflies' were pretty little girls, 'diver boat' meant a lugger, 'peacock' if you saw a young woman in pretty clothes, 'Mrs Moon' if you saw a married woman or a pregnant lady. This was the way we interpreted how we would place our bets. I was really good at cheefah, perhaps I was good at reading the signs.

When Taba came by, Mum would call out, 'You kids got anything to bet, you had a dream?'

Pearl or I might have had a dream about a frog or whatever, so Mum would use that. It might be three shillings, so if you won, the banker would pay odds. There were two draws each day, one at midday and the other at seven in the evening, and when the banker was ready to open the tin, betting would close and everybody would be ready and waiting.

'Hooray!' someone would scream out.

'Bloody shit! I wanted to put that on and I changed it at the last minute,' someone else would scream out.

All around town people would be anxiously waiting.

'Apa kuluar?' people would cry out, wanting to know the answer to the riddle.

If the cheefah man came down our street we would get so excited, wondering which house he would go into. Goodness knows how honest it was. The banker was the only one who knew what was going on, and it was in his hands to select the number and give out the mundei.

I remember one man who used to run the cheefah. Baldhead Tailor was Chinese, and he really was Humpty Dumpty with fat bandy legs. Some kids even called him 'Eggs on Legs'. He had a round head, with a smiley face, and his skin was an egg colour. Some

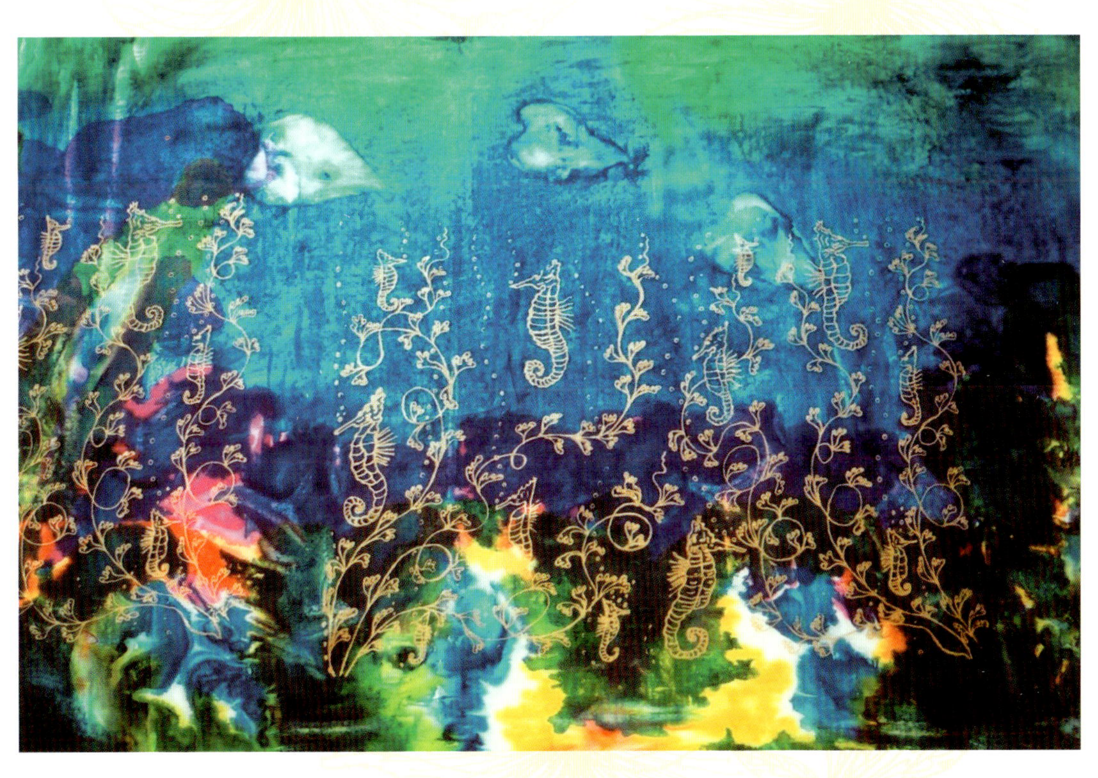

Seahorses Feeding

of the other kids used to call him 'Full-moon Rising'. Baldhead Tailor was a pleasant old man, and he lived in one of the alleyways behind Sun Pictures. He was one of two Chinese tailors in Broome. Mr Dep was the other one and they were both cheefah bankers.

There were always cheefah men working with Baldhead Tailor. Hassan Kling was an Indian, and he was a black clone of his boss. We always found him difficult to understand as he spoke quickly with a strong Indian accent.

There was also Kechel ('small' in Malay), an elf-like Chinese man who lived in Chinatown. We called him 'Kichi', but his real name was Kwok Kwan. We used to tease Kichi because of his size. He would sit with the children on the garden seats at Sun Pictures because he was too small to sit in the deckchairs. We would even use him to measure ourselves, and we really knew we were getting taller when we started looking down at Kichi! Naturally he was very defensive, and sometimes he would get really savage and chase us away.

Taba, an Indonesian cheefah man, used to frighten us and pull faces.

'I'm coming to get you', he'd growl.

Needless to say we didn't tease him because he got in first and scared us away. One of the Chinese cheefah men had a bike so he was one step ahead of the others who had to walk. The cheefah men were very territorial and would get stroppy if someone tried to sell in their area. If Kichi came near our place and we bought our tickets from him, Taba would complain bitterly.

'What for he come here … he not 'sposed to come this way.'

The cheefah men received commission for every ticket they sold. There were no pensions, so the more they sold, the more they made. If they sold the winning ticket, they were paid ten percent by the winner, and that was enough for them to live on. They were up early and selling tickets around town by seven in the morning, ready for the midday draw. If it was a king tide and we'd missed Taba, or if we'd won, we'd have to wade over to Baldhead Tailor's place to pick up our winnings.

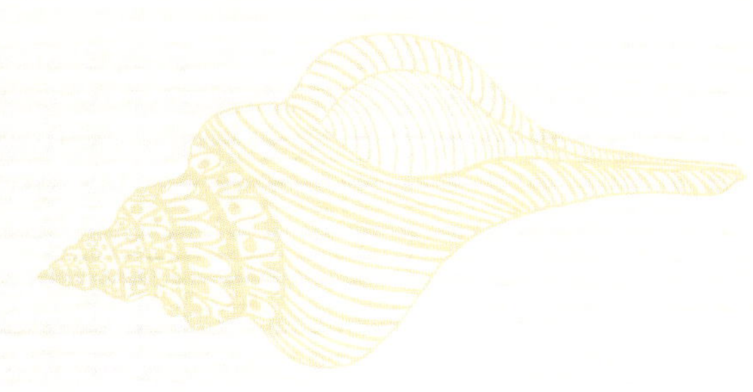

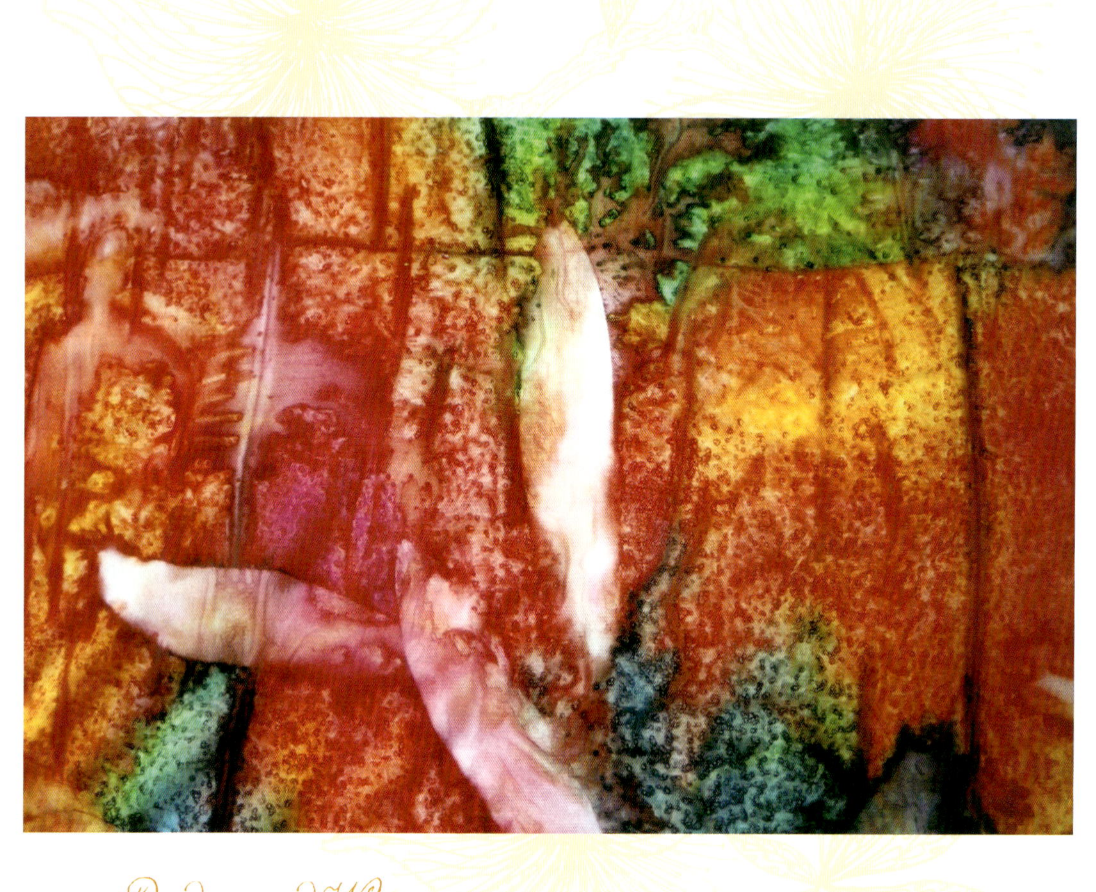

Pindan and Wongai

Fashion

People in Broome were very conscious of fashion. The pearling masters dressed in white, and almost all of the men wore panama hats. Some even wore helmet-style hard hats. Many of the coloured men were very smart dressers and their style reflected the cosmopolitan flavour of the town. I can especially remember that Uncle Max, Uncle Fabian and Simeon always walked out wearing long-sleeved shirts with cufflinks, cravats and panama hats.

The women wore fashionable dresses with hats, stockings and parasols. My mother was very beautiful with her long, shiny black hair, and photos of her when she was young show her in formal dress, with her hair done up in a modern style. Mr Murakami, the Japanese photographer in Chinatown, would sometimes ask her to

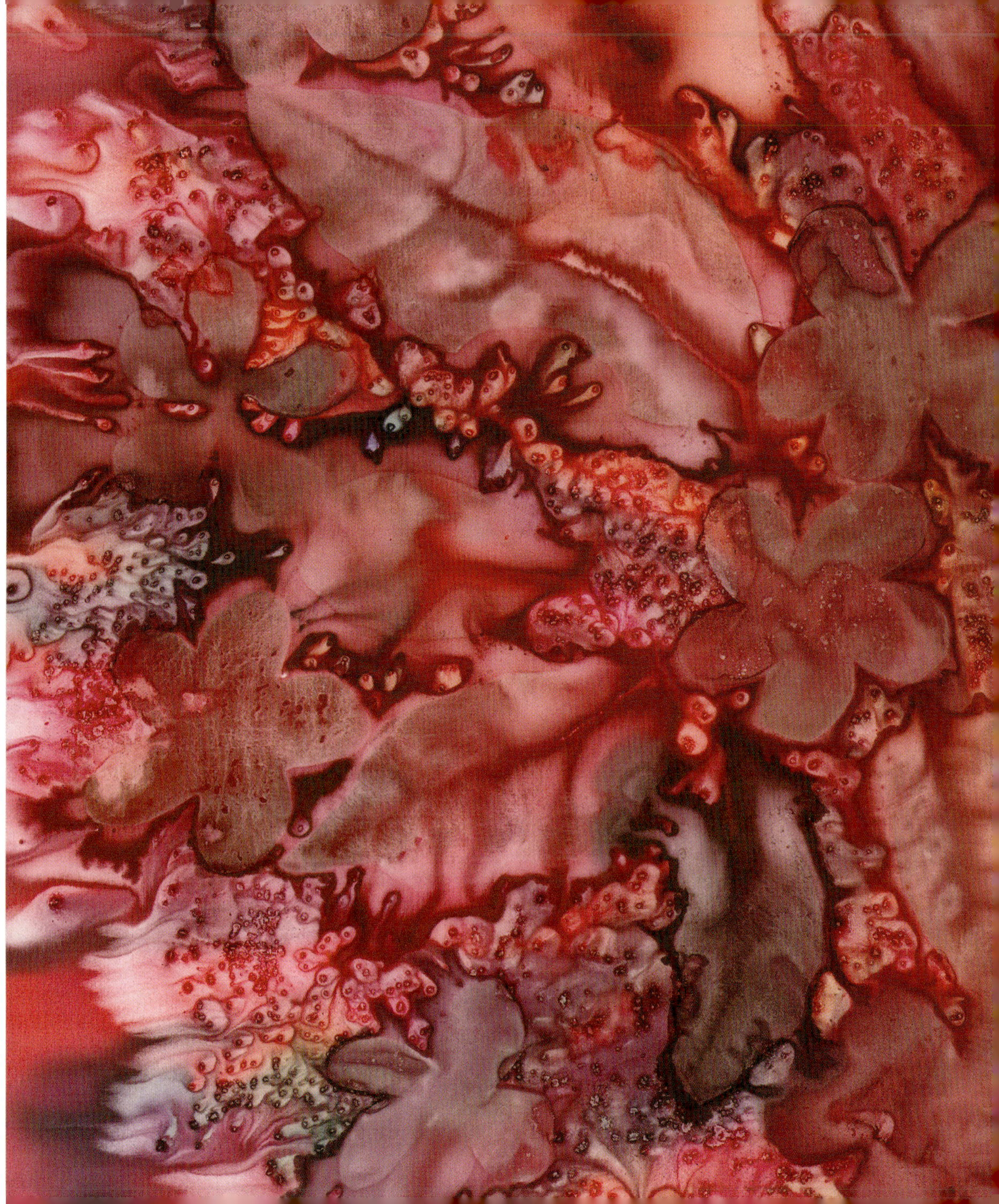

Friends and family

We were taught great respect for our elders and there were many protocols that we had to observe as children. We would always address senior older people either as *Mimi* (grandmother) or *Lulu* (grandfather), and use the term *Datuk* when greeting an elder Malay or Indonesian man.

We would never call anyone our senior by a first name, and people older than us would be referred to as either 'aunty' or 'uncle'. Apart from some of our Melbourne aunties, we would usually greet a European person with either 'Mr', 'Mrs' or 'Miss'. If you saw an older person, you didn't wait for them to greet you. You always greeted them first.

Family is very important to Broome people. My mother would say to Pearl and I, 'You two stick together!' when we were going out to play. Like any younger sister, I wanted what Pearl had. She knew how to dress and I loved looking at her things. When I was nine, I lost my place as the younger sister and Mum began to care for Marietta. Lucy, our cousin, went to Perth to train as a nurse and couldn't take her daughter with her, so Marietta became our little sister. She brought a lot of happiness to our family, and Mum was always grateful that Marietta was never taken away.

There was also our extended family, and we had many aunties and uncles who took care of us. There were my mother's cousins, as well as other older women and men who were friends — black, white, yellow and brown.

Although Simeon was often out at sea, he was an important part of our family and we looked forward to having him home. He always brought treasures like dried seahorses, deep-sea corals, sponges and shells, as well as fish and pearl meat.

Aunty Biddy and Uncle Salem Bin Sallik were also very special in our young lives. Aunty Biddy was my mother's cousin, and after mass on Sunday we'd go to her big house on Weld Street for morning tea or lunch.

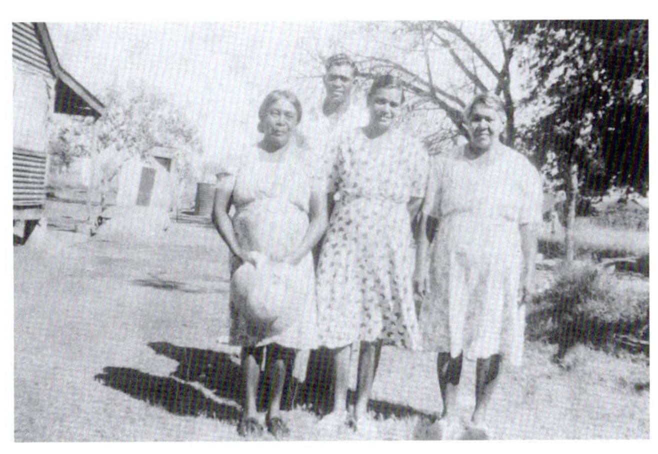

*Aunty Katie Bin Salleh, Richard Corpus,
Mum and Aunty Esther Mustafa, Long House, 1950s.*

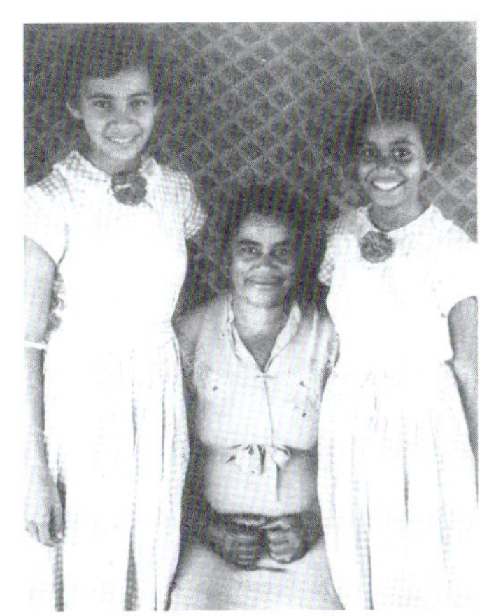

*With Pearl and my mother,
c1953.*

She was a great character and a very learned person — nobody could put one over Aunty Biddy. Her daughter, Mary-Ann, was the same age as Pearl and they were good friends. I loved to play with Mary-Ann's toys, and she was the only one we knew with her own bedroom. Uncle Salem was head diver for McDaniel's and so he earnt a bit more money.

Aunty Esther Mustafa, who we had lived with at the Long House years before, was a regular visitor to our place, and Aunty Katie Bin Salleh came over day and night. She lived across the road with her husband, Achil, and son, Allan, and about twenty cats. Aunties Irene Torres and Agatha Bargas, and Aunties Aggie Dia and Willa, my mother's cousins, came over every afternoon too. They would lounge under a tree, or play a friendly game of cards.

My mother would always look out for other people. She would share our food with people less fortunate, but they would repay her by doing favours, such as chopping the wood or washing clothes. Mimi Emma Corpus lived across the road from us in Robinson Street. When she came over in the evenings, Mum would have a package of food ready. We'd wake some mornings and Mimi Emma would be sitting in our yard weeding the grass. She often took Pearl, myself and the Matsumotos to Magistrate's Beach or to

Buccaneer Rock. We would look for berga berga and cockles as we listened to her stories.

Mum also made friends with her co-workers from the hospital. It wasn't uncommon to have them drop in for a visit. Our house was always open. Sometimes it would seem overcrowded, but Mum would never turn people away.

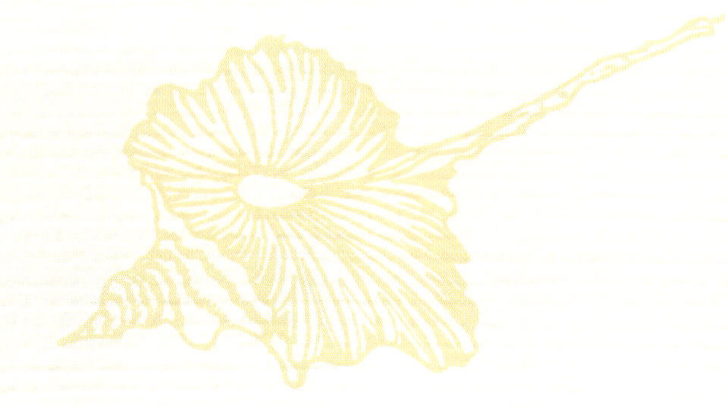

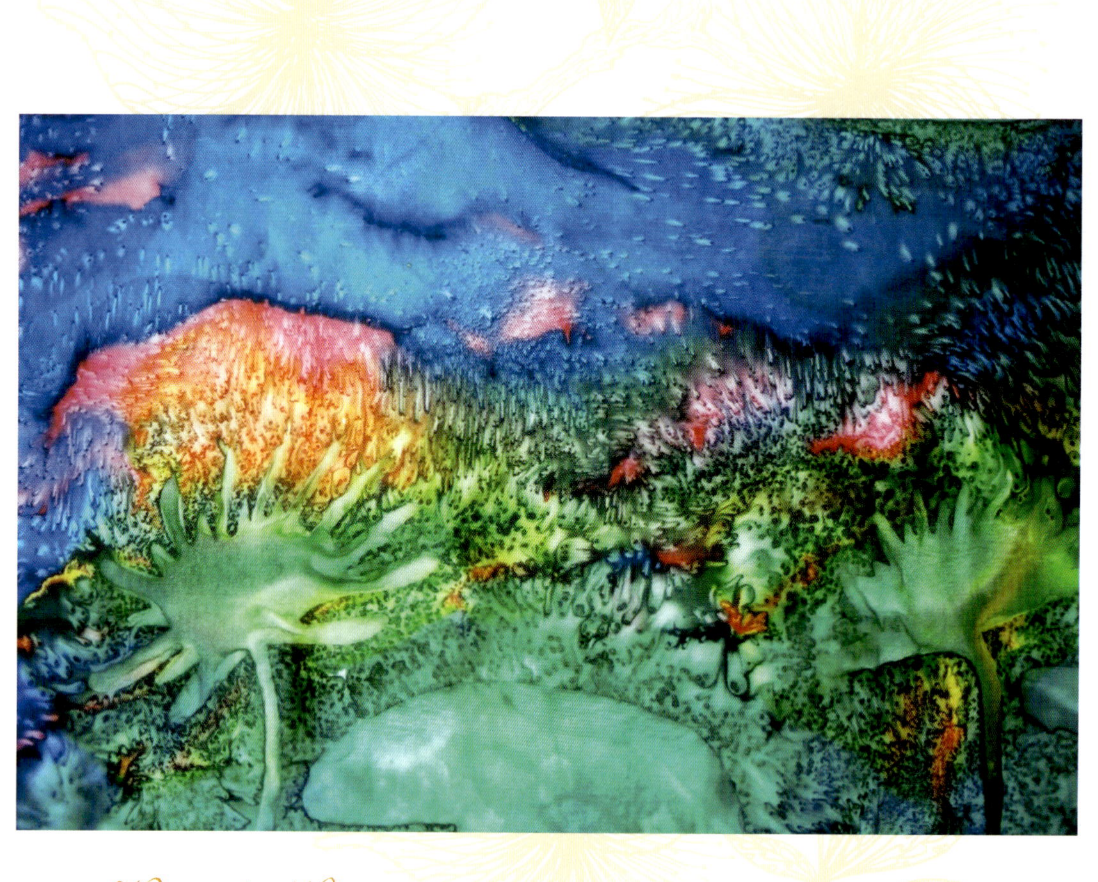

Kimberley Wet

Aunty Bella

Aunty Bella was my mother's only sister and was the aunt I was closest to. She came to live with us in my early teenage years when she finished working at the orphanage.

Aunty Bella never married and she'd say, 'What for you like man, you can do without man!'

She was very independent, and devoted to the church and her work at the orphanage. At the orphanage she was responsible for a whole range of things, including all the sewing, cooking and laundry work.

Because Mum and Aunty Bella were also removed from their families, they had a special feeling for the stolen generation girls from the East Kimberley. Every first Sunday of the month the girls could go out, and Aunty Bella and Mum would take some of them on an outing, especially Phyllis Angela, Maggie Lands, Mary-Anne Sahanna and Patsy Downs. Unlike the kids from the Broome area who had families here, the East Kimberley girls often had no family in town. Aunty Bella and Mum knew how they felt because they had been in the same situation. Those girls, who are now grown women, still say, 'Aunty Bella was the mother we never had.'

Aunty Bella was the greatest storyteller. She always had vivid descriptions of her experiences, and would go into immense detail. Our mouths would water when she described eating food, and we would be thirsty and hungry just listening. One of our favourite stories was when she told us how she used to swim in the billabongs and springs in Beagle Bay. She would dive down and pick the tasty roots of the waterlilies to eat. I had to laugh years later when I tried the roots for myself and found them to be quite bland.

Every night Aunty Bella would make sure that we said our prayers and would sprinkle us kids with Holy Water. Sometimes it was more than a sprinkle, and we would duck under the pillows to stop from being soaked.

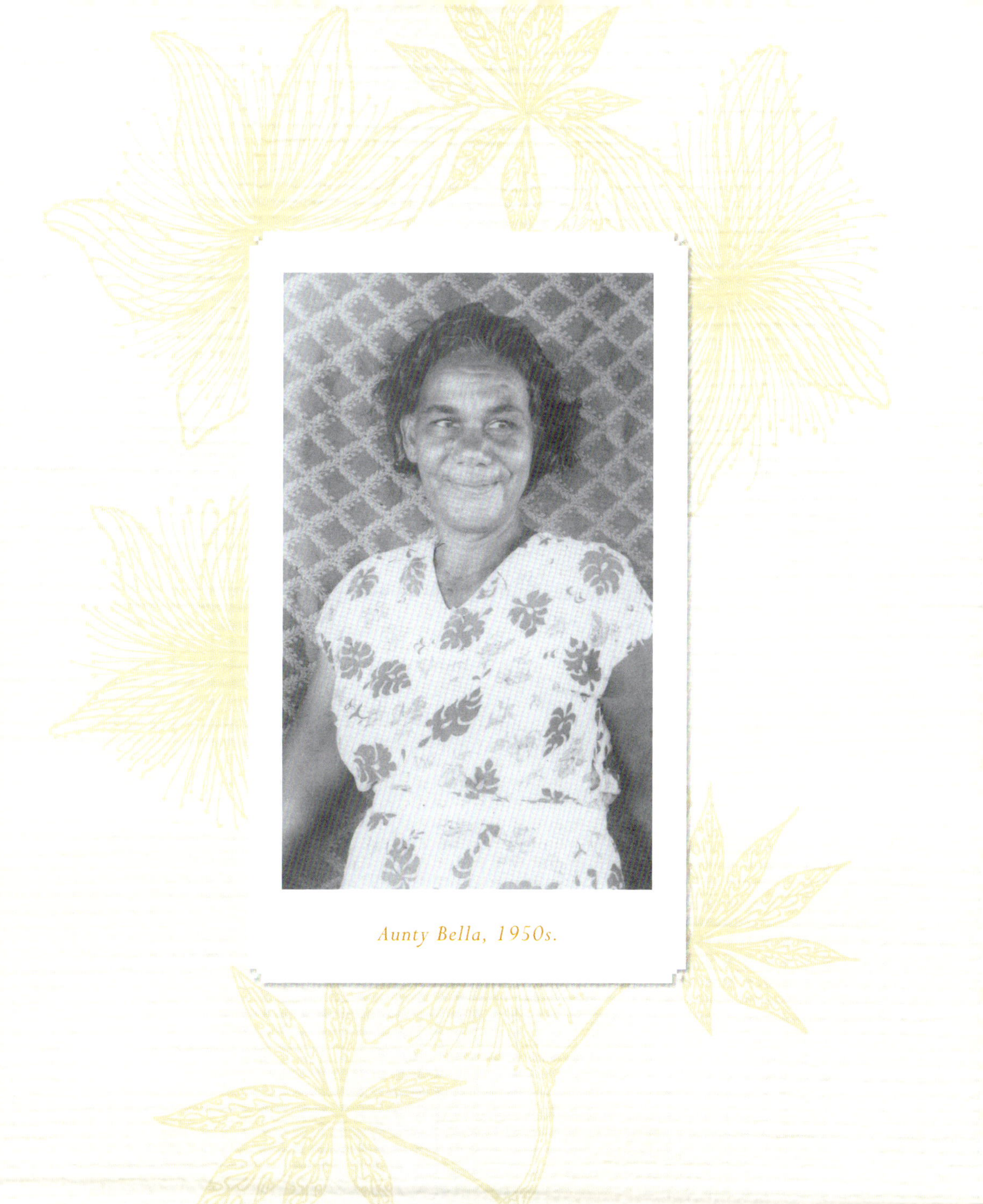

Aunty Bella, 1950s.

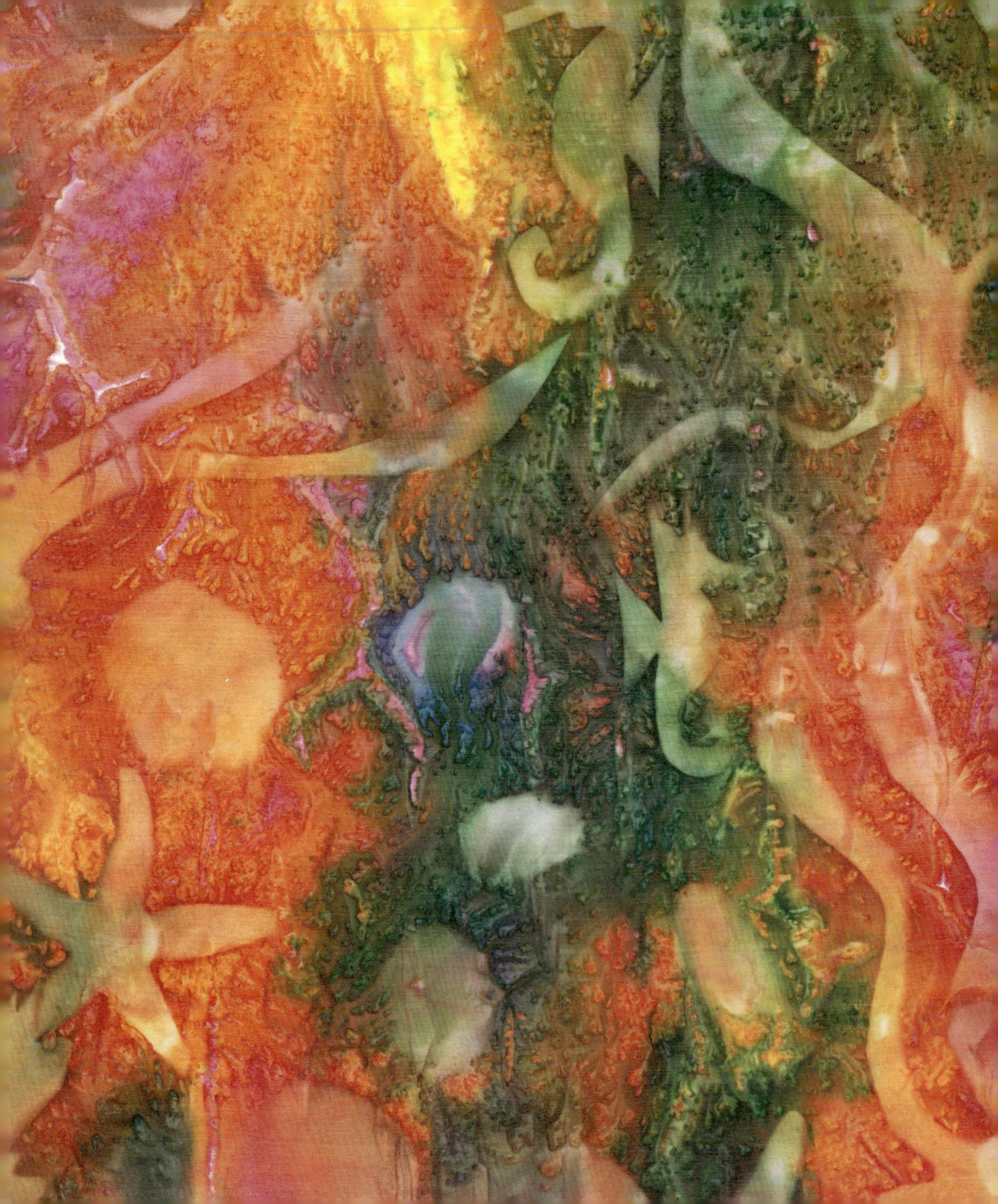

St Mary's

St Mary's Primary School was on Robinson Street behind the Catholic church, Our Lady Queen of Peace Cathedral. The schoolhouse was one big room with a verandah all around, and two doors on each side. The classes went up to year seven and were all taught in the same room. Those who wanted to further their education studied correspondence on the verandah.

My mother was dedicated to the church and she was loyal. There was never a question of where we would be educated. I enjoyed going to school, mostly because of my friends, and we had holidays that the students from Broome Primary School didn't have. Most of the white students in town went to the state school, although there were a few Asians and local families who sent their children there.

The head nun at St Mary's would sit at the top of the hall and closely observe what we were doing. We were all in the same classroom, but at playtime the boys and girls played on opposite sides of the playground — the boys on the left and the girls on the right. Apart from special days there was no mixing of the sexes during playtime. We girls had a huge tamarind tree and a poinciana tree on our side but we weren't allowed to climb them — it wasn't ladylike. There were no school lunches, but every day the government provided tinned 'Carnation Milk' diluted with water. If we had money we would go across the road to Ellies' shop and buy ice-blocks or lollies.

Lunch was the big meal of the day and most of us went home for it. When we were living near the airport it was a long walk home, especially on hot days. We didn't have shoes or thongs, but some kids had leather sandals. If you couldn't afford shoes, you went barefoot. So we'd be jumping from one piece of grass to the next. If you had sandals you would stand on a piece of grass and throw them back for the next person to walk on. We'd try and share with someone close to our foot size. Sometimes we tied cardboard to our feet with string.

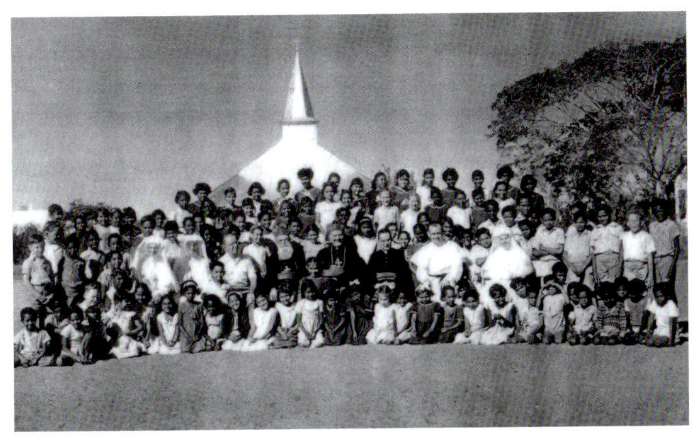

St Mary's students with the nuns, priests and visiting clergy. Bishop Raible, with the beard, is in the second row. Note the 'blue army' girls in their uniforms, c1956.

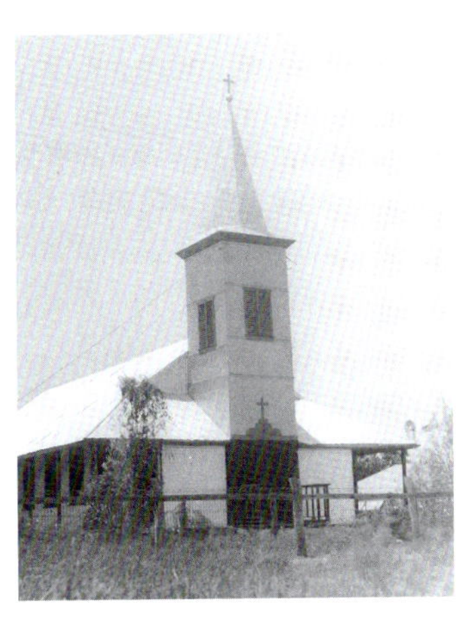

The first Catholic Church in Broome.

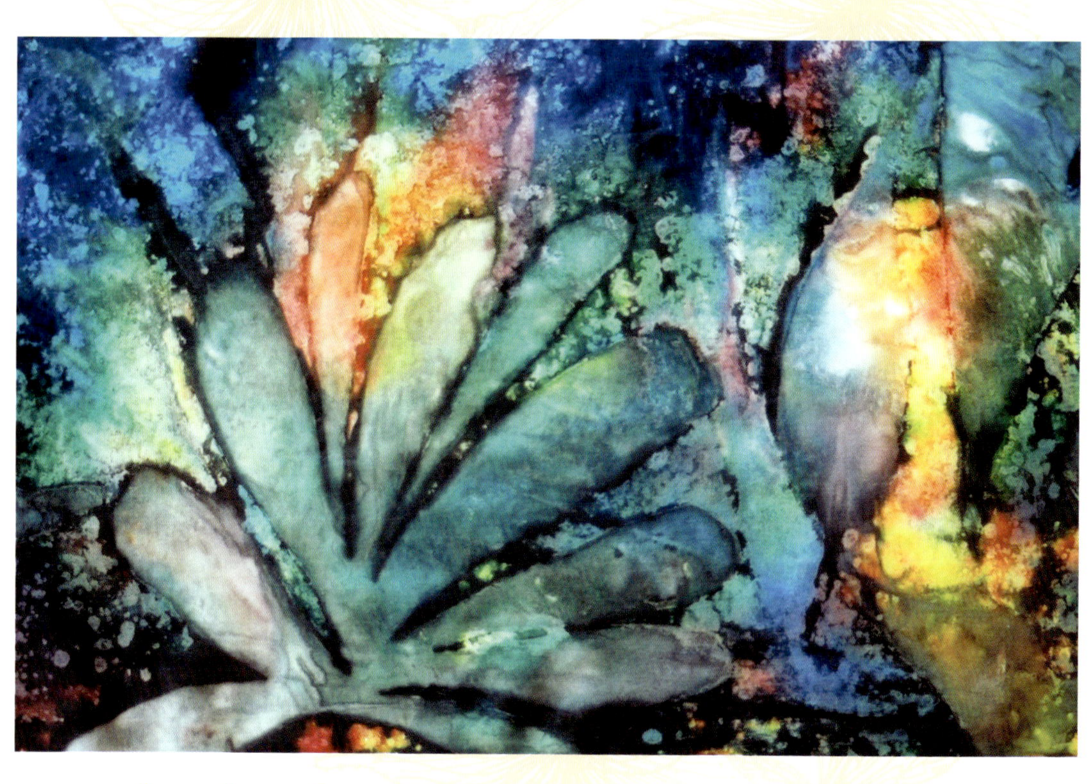

Sea Star Dreaming

St Mary's was famous for its sport. On Friday afternoons the boys competed against the state school in cricket and football and they usually won. The girls played softball, and we sometimes had mixed games with the boys. At playtime we played games like rounders and hopscotch.

The interschool sports between St Mary's and the state school was held during race week. Wednesday was Ladies Bracelet, and the Broome Cup was the following Monday. School sports day was held on the Sunday. There were running races, long jump and high jump, and ball games like softball, tunnel ball, pass ball and leader ball.

We all loved to cheer on our school team, and most of the children loved the sports carnival, but not me. I wasn't good at athletics and preferred team sports. Even though I hated it, I had to join in. My good friend, Bernadette Puertollano, and I took it in turns to be last or second last. We'd try and hide because we knew we would get teased by the other kids.

Team sports were much more fun for me, and I used to play netball. Elsta Roe was the captain, and apart from a few of us, the rest of the girls had all left school. It was a highlight when we played against Derby. When it was their race weekend we would travel up to Derby for a game, and likewise, they would come down during our race week.

In 1954, the first Kimberley Camp School was held and it was one of the highlights of my school life. Children came from throughout the Kimberley and as far away as the Pilbara. The out-of-towners camped at the state school, but we went along each day. We began with a roll call, and then we were given our timetable and put into groups.

It was wonderful, but there was one thing that caused us shame — we had to wear bloomers while the other girls wore shorts! Our only consolation was that St Mary's won *all* the games. At night the entertainment was at the Shire Hall. We did ballroom dancing, barn dances and all sorts.

'Sides together right … sides together left … sides together right … left … sides together both.'

All the girls had a ball and we behaved like typical twelve-year-old girls just discovering boys. A few of us had a crush on a boy from Port Hedland, and I got the biggest thrill when he sent a message through one of my friends that he wanted to sit next to me at the pictures on Saturday night. We sat and held hands during the film, and the other girls were quite envious!

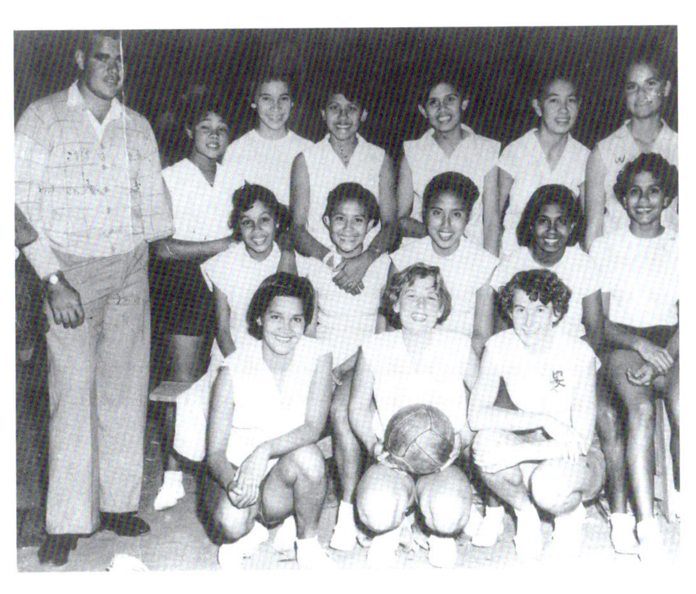

Our netball team — Coach, Charlie Martin, Theresa Torres, Pearl, Louise Roe, Janet Rajak, Clare Bargas, Mary-Anne Martin, myself, Mary Rose Lee, Eileen Matsumoto, Louise Torres (dec), Lorraine Buckle, Rosie Hunter, Jennifer Merritt, Kathy Franklin, c1953.

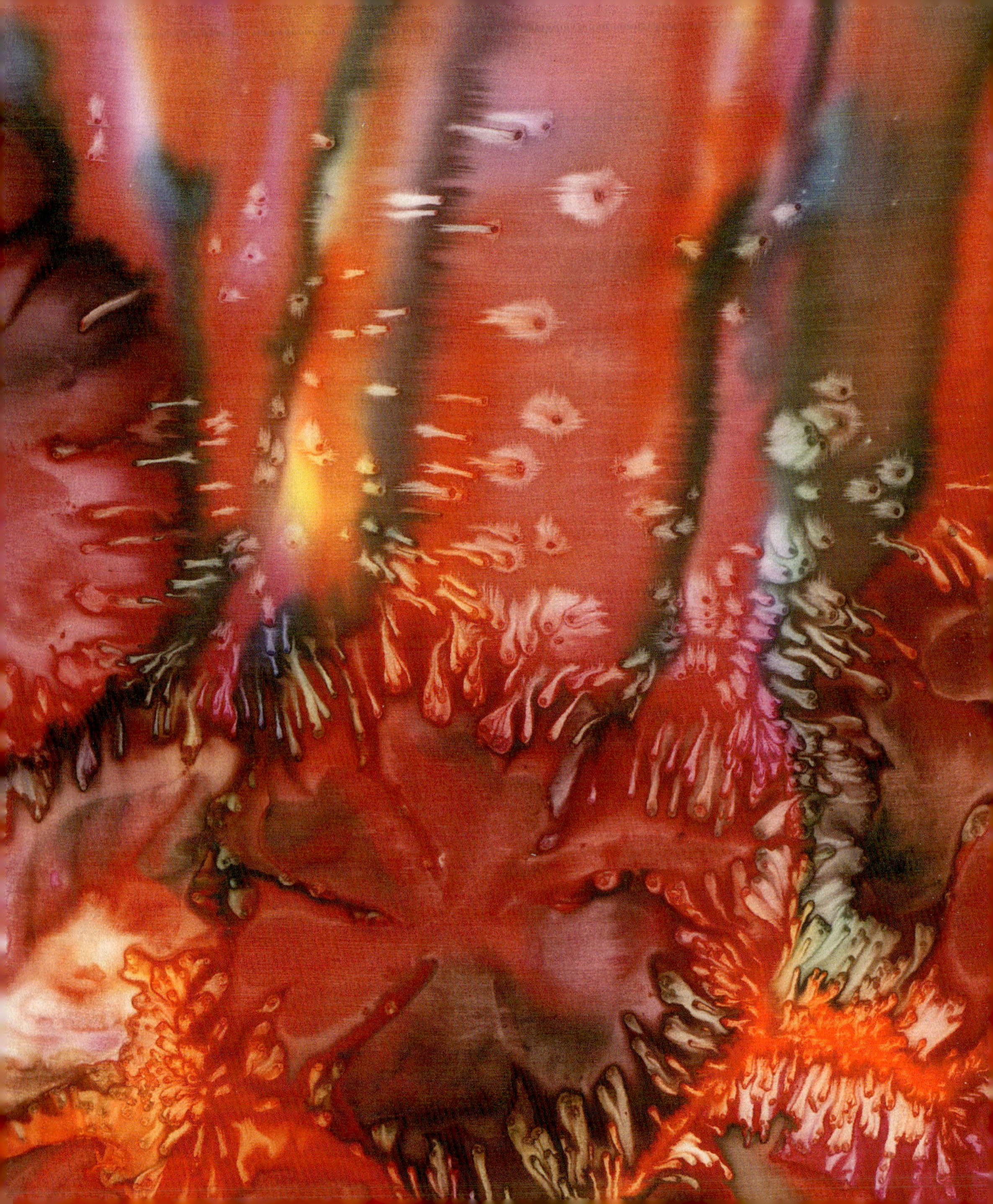

The Nuns

The St John of God Sisters were our teachers. They were trained as nurses but they were also excellent teachers. Some of them were quite strict and, boy, did they drum it in! Sister Catherine taught us the basics — reading, writing and arithmetic. After morning prayers she would make us sit, take a deep breath, and then go straight into mental arithmetic. If we didn't get ten out of ten, we had to do our tables at home that night. If we got a word wrong in spelling, we had to write it out ten times, or until we learnt it. If there was anything we didn't learn in class, then we did it for homework, and the next day we were given a test.

When I first started school we wrote all our work onto a small slate with chalk. Once the nuns had checked it, we'd rub it off with our little duster and begin our next lesson. At the end of the day, we wiped the slates clean with a damp cloth. As I moved up the grades, the school introduced paper, pen and ink. Each desk had a little ink-pot, and we would dip the nib in and write our lessons. It taught us to write neatly as we had to hold the pen in the proper way, or the nuns would slap our fingers. The desks were arranged in straight rows, and we sat with our eyes to the front. We certainly never called out or answered back. The nuns were strict and they wanted us to learn.

Reading on the verandah was fun. There were different age levels in the room so we would move our chairs outside, and take turns reading to the teacher. We read Rudyard Kipling, Hans Christian Andersen and other folk tales. The nuns made sure we read good literature, and 'The Little Match Girl' was one of my favourites. I'd be sitting in the Broome heat shivering, as I imagined her in the snow without any family or friends.

Mother Raymond was one of my first teachers. She was a very old nun, and she would sit up at her table, look out over her glasses and try to keep awake.

'Don't yawn,' she would say.

Well, Mother Raymond had some kind of sleeping sickness

and so we would yawn, and then she would yawn. This would go on until her eyes closed and she dropped off to sleep. When she was asleep we would start misbehaving.

We held some wonderful concerts with the nuns, and the whole town looked forward to these performances. We would rehearse for weeks and door-knock around the town selling tickets.

We did all kinds of dancing, as well as ballets like the 'Pink Lady', and we performed plays like 'Snow White' and 'Sleeping Beauty'. The boys were very agile and they did gymnastic displays performing impressive feats such as five-high pyramids, somersaults, vaulting over the wooden horse, and walking on their hands.

When Sisters Joan Mansfield and Leone Collins came to Broome, we could relate to them better than the older nuns. They were young postulants and we saw them being professed. Sister Joan was a wonderful singer and dancer and she taught us ballet, folk dancing and singing. We learnt the Maypole, which we did every Christmas, and dances for the concerts like the 'Sailor's Hornpipe', the 'Highland Fling', and the 'Sword Dance'.

Sister Catherine was a small, fiery nun from Melbourne, and

she would get us to perform songs like 'I Love a Sunburnt Country' to stir up our patriotic feelings. Sometimes we got the giggles when we mixed up our singing rounds, and Sister Catherine did not enjoy these antics at all.

Mother Ignatius was one of our most interesting sisters. She was very dignified, a natural-born teacher, and a true environmentalist. She loved taking us out bush for nature studies, and we'd all set off to Willie Creek or Denim Station. We'd look for birds, observe their appearance and habits, and then describe them back to her. We discovered *dindi* (mud larks), bowerbirds, emus, black cockatoos and many other species. Sometimes we studied the local flora, or she would take us to the beach to learn about shells and the different types of rocks and sand.

On one trip out to Gantheaume Point, she pointed to the ocean and asked, 'What's that?'

'The sea,' I replied confidently.

'No, what's that?' she repeated.

'Blue,' I said, this time feeling a bit less confident.

'No, the Indian Ocean is the correct answer!'

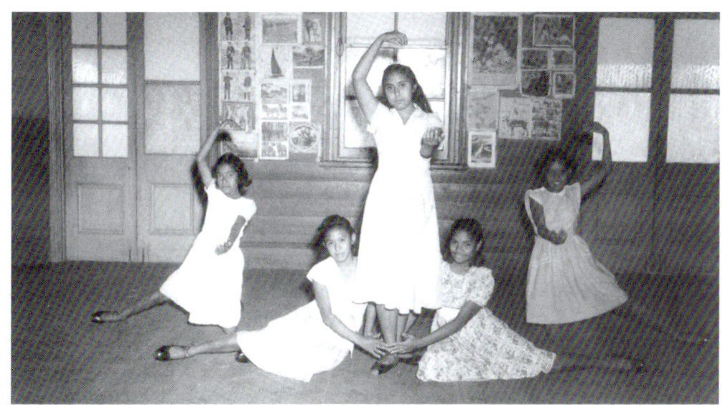

Pauline Mamid (dec), Mary Rose Lee, Eileen Matsumoto (pink lady), Bernadette Puertollano, and myself performing the 'Pink Lady' ballet, choreographed by Sr Joan Mansfield, 1953.

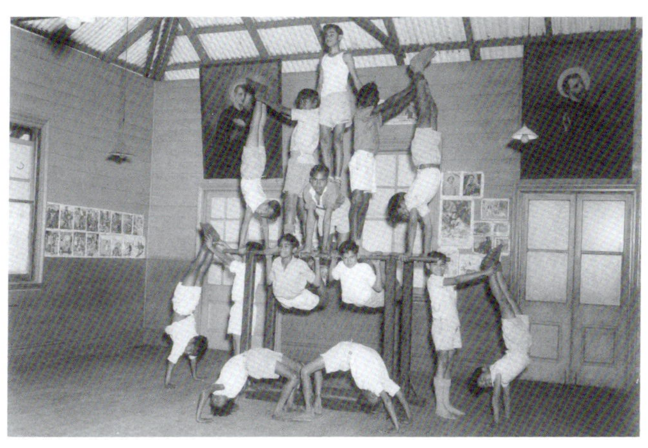

The boys performing one of their gymnastic displays, 1953.

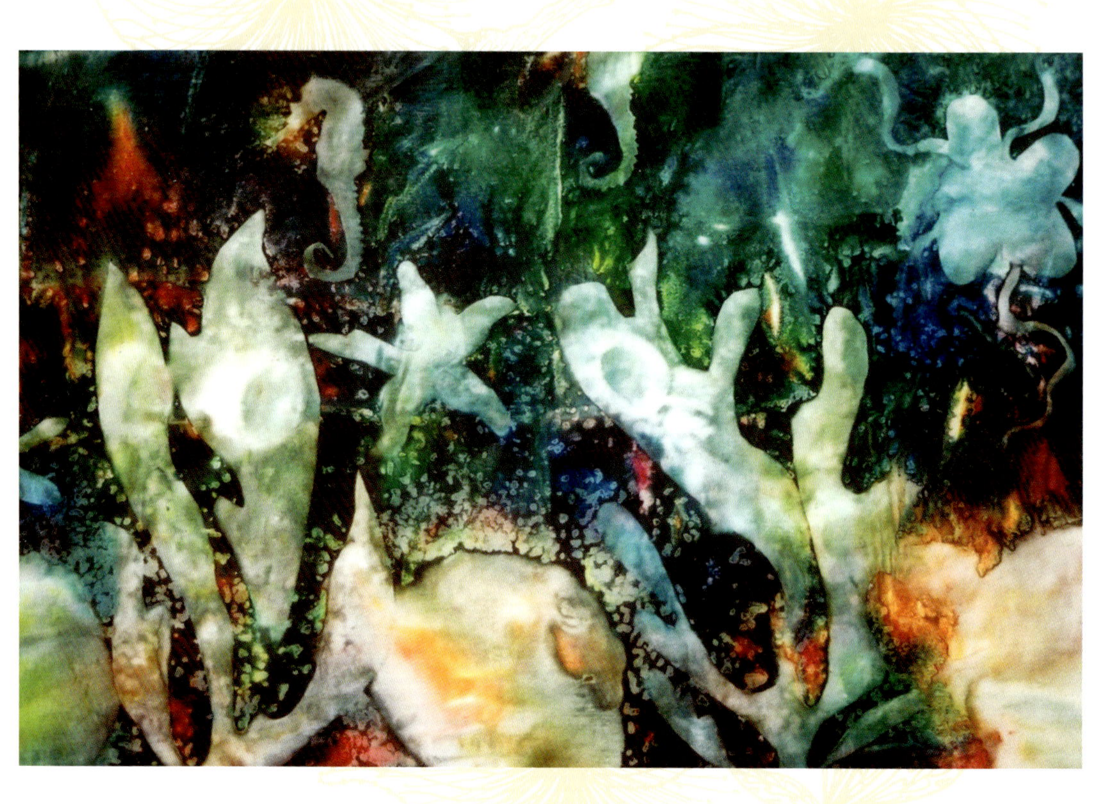

Seahorses Playing

When we learnt about geography and history, she would get out maps and point out countries of the world and their capital cities. She would make us learn the names of cities, and their former names.

'Name a city in Turkey.'

'Istanbul.'

'What was it called before?'

'Constantinopole!'

Mother Ignatius taught elocution, too. We had to pronounce our words properly.

See the blue sky on Tuesday. Betty Boo all dressed in blue.
A E I O U.

We would form the words slowly and with great care, and use our fingers to hold the right position in our mouths. We also recited poetry. The poem, 'If', by Rudyard Kipling was one of her favourites.

In the morning we did exercises in deportment and breathing. 'Breathe in, shoulders back. Take a deep breath.' We stood in line and held our hands out in front of us so she could check our fingernails. If they were dirty, we got a whack across our fingers. It really hurt, especially on cold mornings, but it did encourage us to keep our hands washed and our hair tied back — girls with a ribbon and boys with trimmed hair. We didn't have uniforms, we just wore ordinary clothes, but we had to have sleeves — cotton frocks with sleeves. If our dresses had no sleeves, we would be sent home. It didn't matter if your clothes were raggedy, they just had to be clean. 'Cleanliness' was her key word. During lessons we sat like ladies with our legs closed, crossed at the ankles and no slouching. Sister Ignatius would tap our backs to straighten us up.

When we were naughty, the nuns would sometimes make us do the weeding. We would use a hoe or a shovel, or weed with our bare hands. One time I nearly spewed. I was weeding and a big, green caterpillar squashed in my hands. It was hard work, and if you were given a patch to weed, you had to stay until it was finished.

One very strict rule Sister Catherine had was *no* chewing. There was a girl who chewed gum all the time, and she often chewed the whole packet at once.

'This is your last chance! If you keep on chewing, I'm going to have you in front of the class and wrap that chewing gum over you.'

Eventually the girl did get caught and she had to kneel down in front of the class. Sister Catherine took the gum out of her mouth and wrapped it around her face and hair.

She wasn't the only one to get in trouble though. Once I wrote a note about how we all called Sister Catherine, 'Shorty', and I threw it across the room to a friend. Sister Catherine picked it up and read it to the whole class. She then challenged the girls to admit whether anyone else called her names. It must have been a full five minutes before some of them began to stand up. Not only did I get the 'strap', but some of the other girls were punished as well.

The school and convent buildings were spread out and there was no telephone. The teacher would ask, 'Who wants to take a message for me to the convent?' and we would all put our hands up. Everybody loved running a message across to the convent because Sister Veronica would be at the kitchen door, and she was a wonderful cook. She would usually give us a piece of bread or a freshly baked biscuit. I loved the smells coming from that kitchen.

We all did art. Most of the children were good artists, but I didn't think I was. I used to get my cousin, Maureen, to draw my horse or whatever, and I would help her with her sums. We used greasy crayons and got excited if we were able to use watercolour paints. We sometimes got paints for prizes, and I did win a prize for one drawing. I drew the poles under the jetty, and I had seagulls sitting along the rail. I never thought then that I would grow up to be an artist.

The nuns always encouraged us to 'Read! Read! Read!' and to take books home. Some nights we had to read the school paper because it contained all the news, but I think I got my true love of reading from my mother. Although she had some schooling at Beagle Bay, Mum educated herself by reading. She could talk about any subject.

I must have read too much in bad light during these years, because I started wearing heavy glasses when I was older. We only had DC power, with orange light, and we used pencil torches to read at night. My mother would turn the lights off and then I'd pull out my little torch and read until two or three in the morning.

'Sally, you gonna be blind before you are even old!' she'd yell.

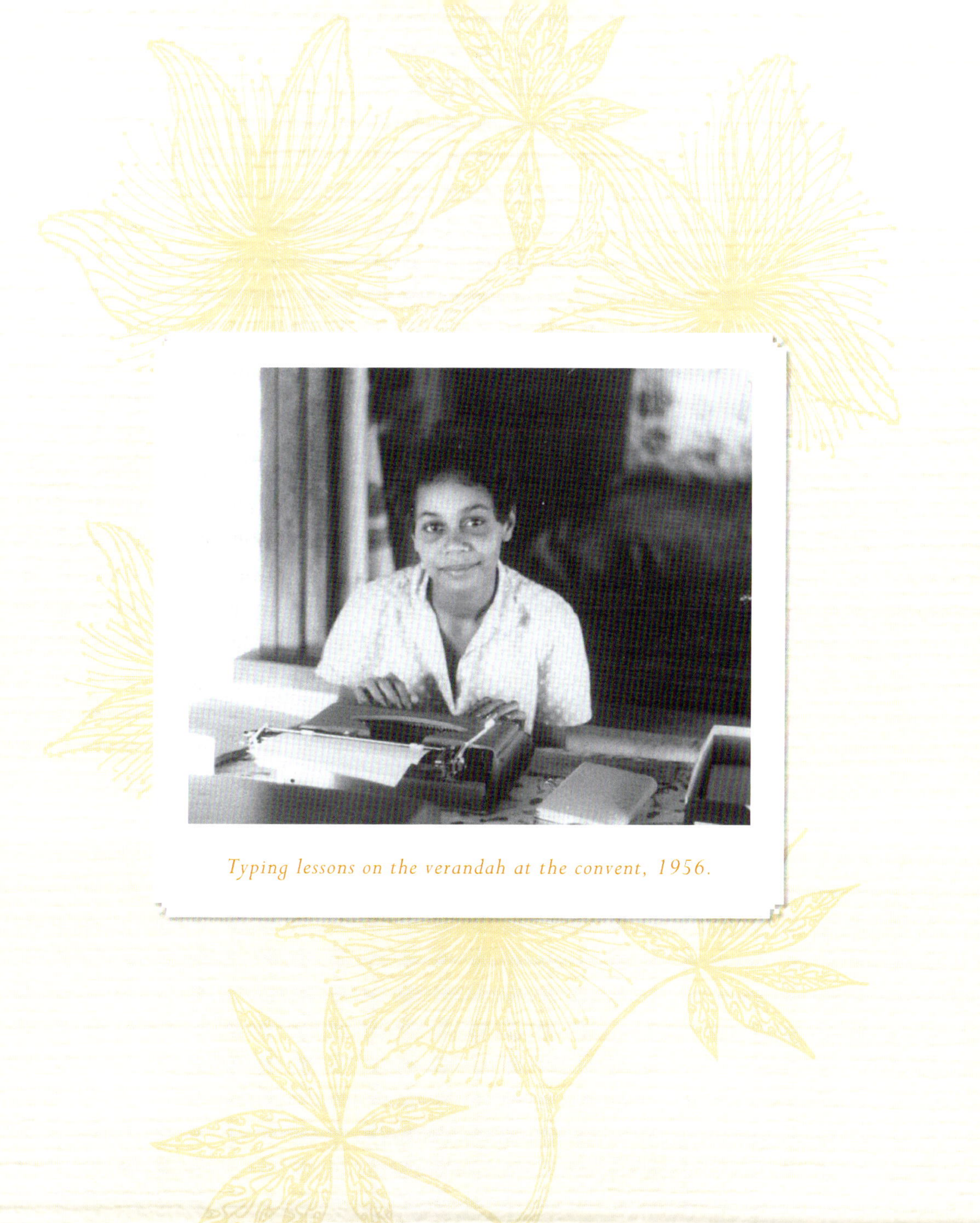

Typing lessons on the verandah at the convent, 1956.

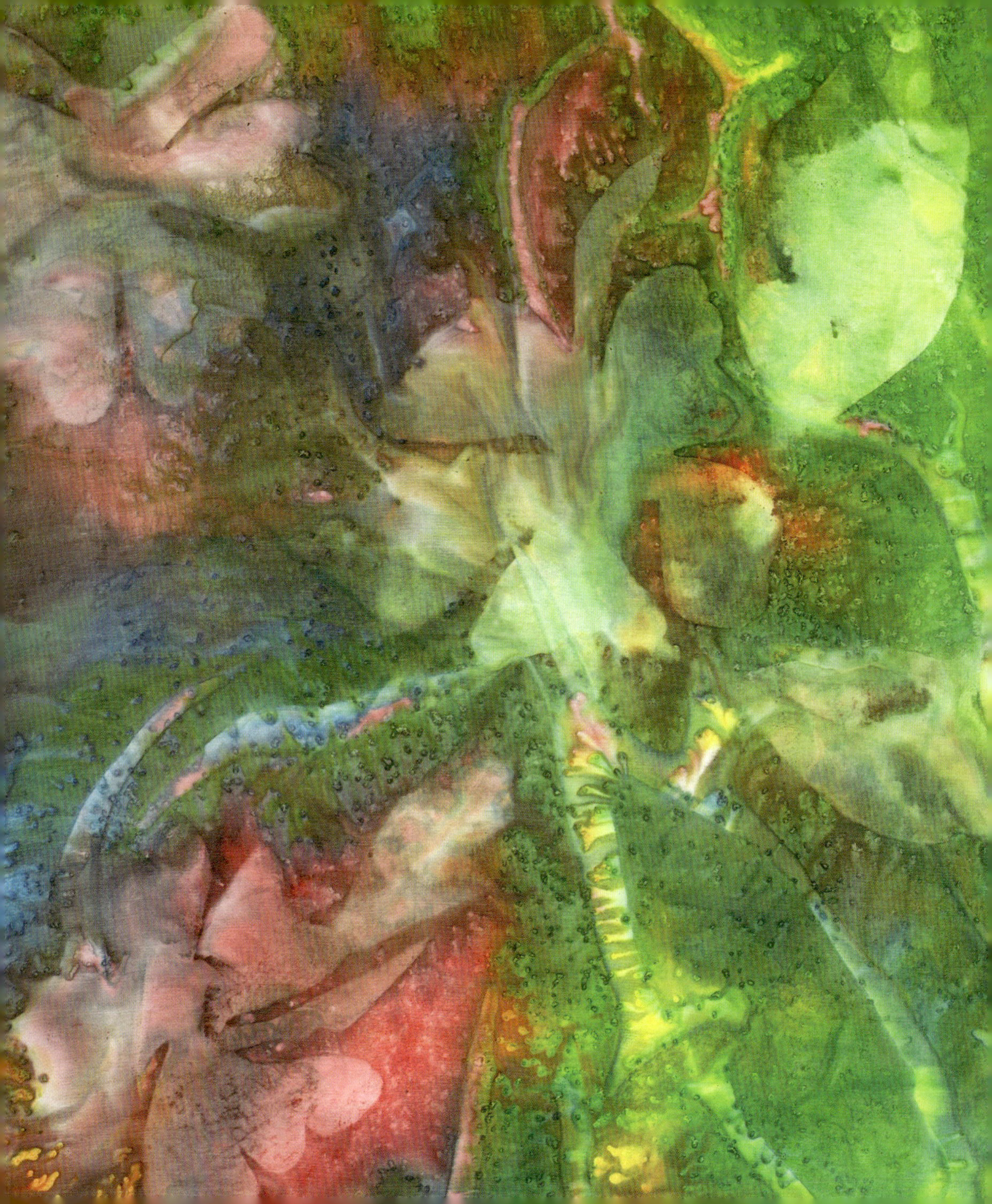

Getting sick

My worst childhood sickness was tonsillitis, which I got about three times a year, or when the weather changed. I tried getting them out when I was younger but the doctors said it wasn't a safe procedure. We'd get needles for polio and whooping cough. Whooping cough was bad and I can still remember hearing people with that awful cough.

Once when Simeon was out at sea, a bad flu hit and we were all lying flat on our backs — Mum, Pearl, Marietta, and myself — but usually Mum, or one of our aunties, would treat us when we were ill. We grew up with Asian remedies like 'Tiger Balm' and we used it for all ailments. The oil *minyah geliga*, we got from Singapore. It was used for many sicknesses, and I still use it for all manner of things from indigestion to massage. Mum also made us take cod liver oil or some other tonic every morning.

At times, measles, chickenpox and mumps were rife. Pearl, Marietta and myself all got measles at the same time. In our house on Robinson Street, we usually slept in the sleep-out, but Mum moved us into the darkest room because the sleepout was flooded with light. Because measles makes your eyes light sensitive, we needed the darkness. The sleep-out had flywire but it was riddled with holes and we slept under mosquito nets.

On my twelfth birthday, I was once again at home with tonsillitis, burning up with a fever under the mosquito net. Mum was working at the hospital and because we only lived two houses down, she would pop home to see if I was alright. I thought I was going to die that day.

Another memorable time was when I was sick on the day of a school picnic. Mum didn't want me to go but I complained so much that I got my own way. I ended up having a terrible time and lay huddled on a blanket the entire day. I should have listened to my mother, but I would do anything to go on a school picnic.

One of my greatest fears came to fruition when I was bitten by a snake. We carried torches at night because the streetlights were poor, and one evening Mum, Pearl and myself were walking by over to my cousin's house along a little track, when I felt a sharp nip along the side of my foot.

'Snake, snake!' I screamed.

We quickly ran into my cousin's house, and on closer inspection, they found two fang marks. They cut the bite with a razor, and since Mum couldn't suck the blood out because of her bad teeth, my cousin had to suck it out instead. Three houses down there was a taxi driver, Jack Lee, who ran us to the hospital. Thankfully, within a couple of days I was feeling much better.

The old Broome hospital was a long, narrow building with wide verandahs. The wards were big rooms lined with beds, and if they were full, the patients slept on the verandahs. When I was there, so was old Sam Sui. He was an old Chinese man who used to clean shell. He had lost an eye when he got shell grit in it, and he now had a glass eye. One night I heard old Sam Sui yelling out.

Hearing a commotion, the nurse came down the verandah with a torch, 'What's wrong, Sam?'

'My eye, my eye. I can't find my eye!' he shouted back.

The Native Hospital, or the Back Hospital as we called it, was on Dora Street. The Front Hospital (Broome District Hospital) was for Europeans and people with citizenship. I remember noticing when I went to visit my teenage cousin who was dying of tuberculosis, that the staff at the Native Hospital were all white.

Sickness and death were a part of our lives and people were scared of infections and illnesses that they knew had caused deaths in the past. Penicillin had just come in, but the medical services in town were pretty basic and it was not an easy trip to get to Perth.

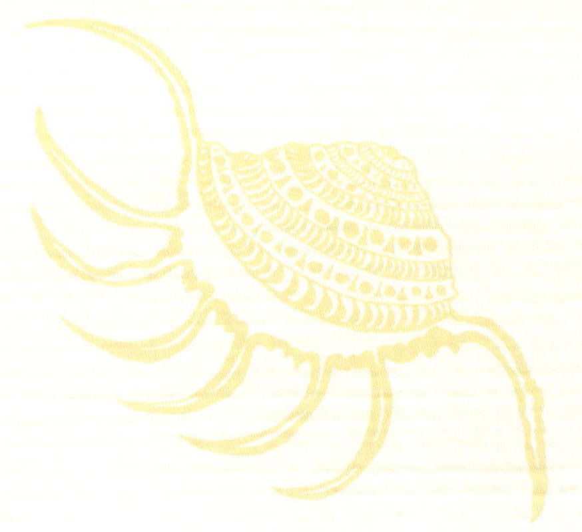

Cyclone of 1957

I left school, in April 1956, as soon as I turned fourteen. We were still living in the house on Robinson Street and it was time to help Mum out and contribute to the family income. Luckily I was able to get a job at Streeter & Male in Chinatown, serving ice-cream and squash on the front verandah.

Town was busy and there were still more than fifty luggers working. Business was steady, especially at smoko and lunchtime, because all the lugger crews would up come for a glass of squash or an ice-cream. It was hard work and some days I must have served over a hundred men. They were usually in a hurry, and would sometimes get impatient and bang on the counter, demanding 'Squashy, squashy!'

Mr de Pedro, my boss, would always keep an eye on me to make sure I wasn't slacking off, but if he saw I was busy, he would send another assistant out to lend a hand. Mr de Pedro was strict and expected absolute punctuality, but he would occasionally show his softer side. Sometimes he would ask me when my birthday was. I would meekly reply and he would say, 'Remind me to buy you a bloody watch.'

Although I was now working, my social circle did not change much and life revolved around family and friends.

The following year, on 14 February, 1957, my cousin, Maureen, was turning sixteen and we were all looking forward to her party. It never happened.

The rain started early that morning, and it was coming down heavy. The verandah around our house was enclosed with shutters but it wasn't long before it was flooded. We moved into the two very small rooms in the middle of the house.

It rained all day. We didn't know it was a cyclone as there were no warnings like you get today. Although there had been light rain for days before, we didn't think much of it. As the day went on,

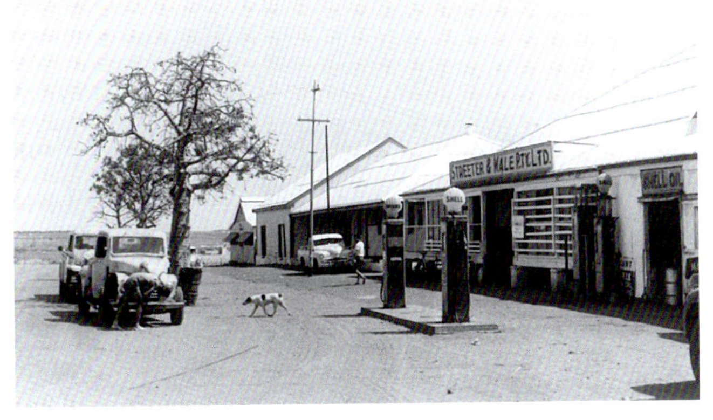

My first job was at Streeter & Male where I sold ice-cream and squash from the verandah.

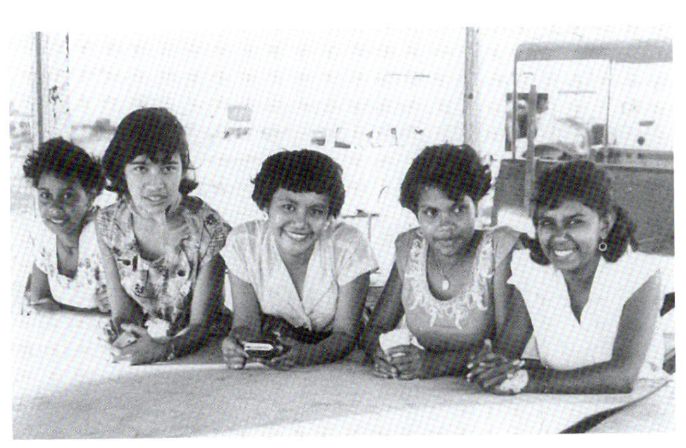

At the Broome races helping the Catholic Church with the catering — myself, Pearl, Mary Rose Lee, Bernadette Puertollano, and Louise Torres (dec), c1957.

the rain and wind intensified and we spent all day and night trapped in the house. Even our safe haven, the two rooms in the middle of the house, were wet as the rain blew in under the doors.

Pearl, Daisy Drummond and I moved into the old bathroom. We weren't sure whether they were the safest places to be, but the bathroom and the kitchen were the driest spots. We looked out towards the west, and laughed our heads off when we saw the neighbours' outhouses falling over one by one. When we saw the overflowing rainwater tanks rolling away, we realised how serious it was!

It wasn't until the rain had stopped, and the wind had eased, that we knew we had been in the middle of a cyclone. The town was devastated and there was damage everywhere. People were running up to the hospital, just down from our house. Then someone came to tell us that Daisy's sister, Annie, had been trapped in a house that had collapsed. Neighbours came and slept in our house that night because houses had lost their roofs. Many of the houses in Broome were old, and not built to stand up to the force of the destructive winds. Annie had survived, but two other people had been killed. I went with Daisy to visit Annie in the hospital and she was badly bruised, her eyes were bloodshot and she was in shock.

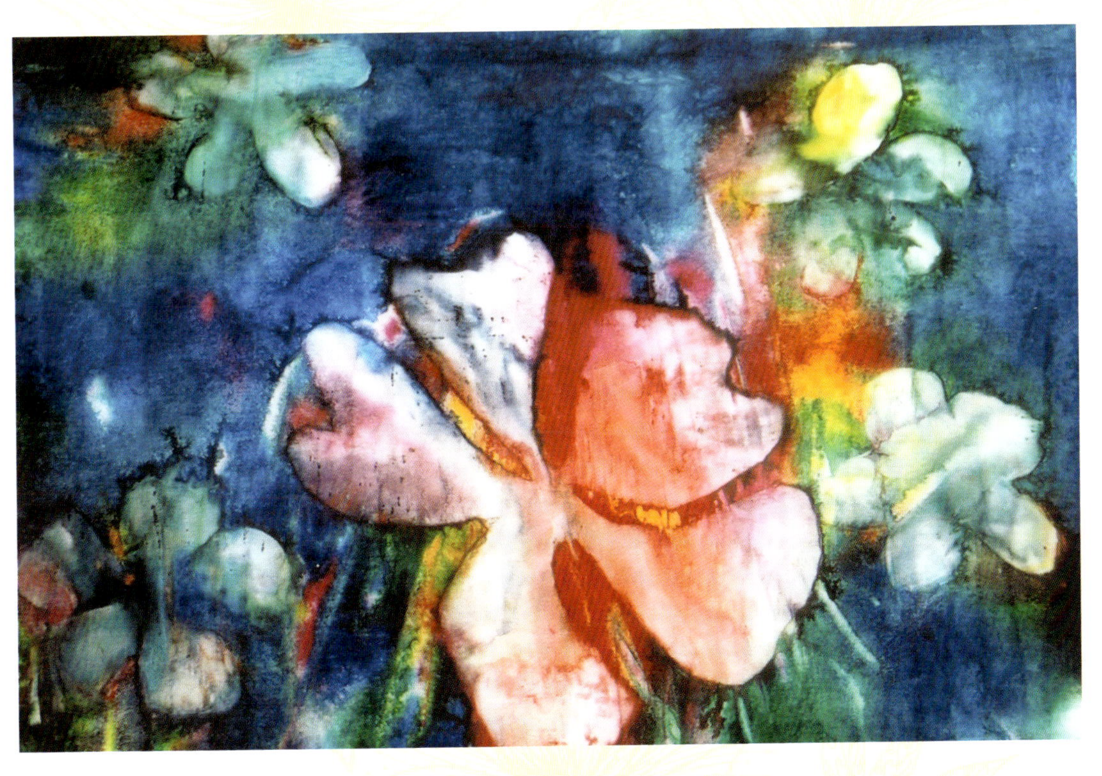

Tropical Bloom 2

The next day I went back to work and Mr de Pedro wanted to know where I had been the day before and why I hadn't turned up. He said it in such a serious voice that to this day I still don't know if he was joking!

I was fourteen years old, and a working girl in my home town. I was a young woman who had been through the dangers of a cyclone, and I was feeling the terrible affects it had on our community. For the first time, I felt as if I was leaving my childhood behind, and that my adult life was beginning.

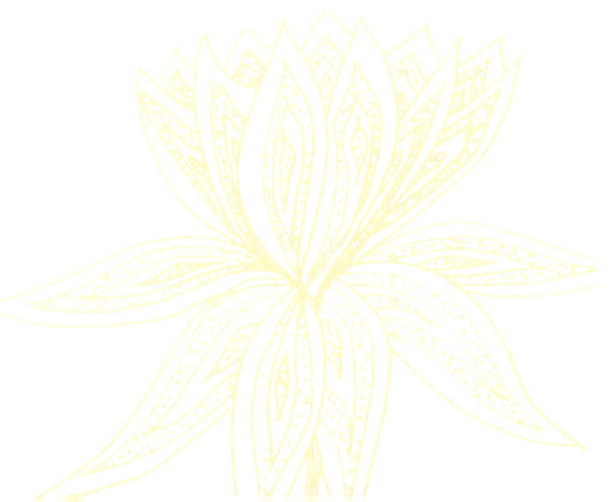

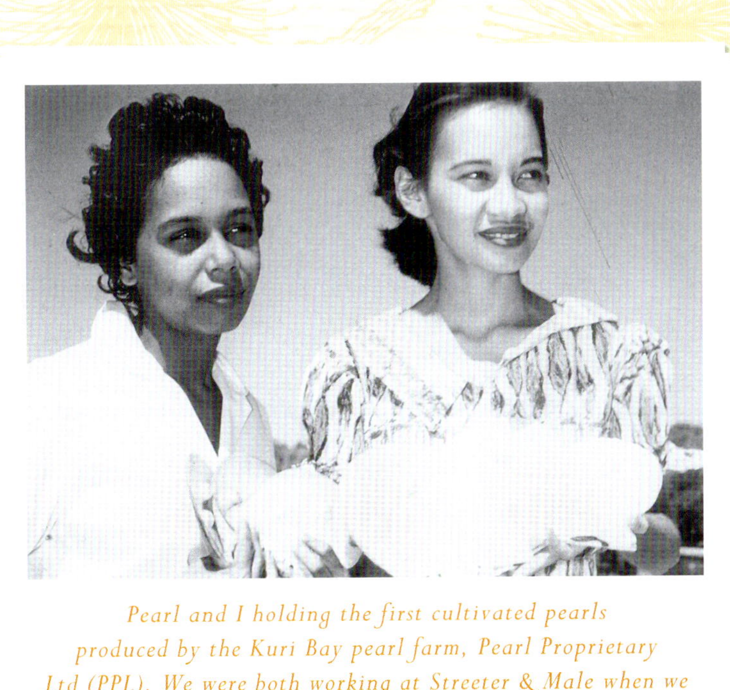

Pearl and I holding the first cultivated pearls produced by the Kuri Bay pearl farm, Pearl Proprietary Ltd (PPL). We were both working at Streeter & Male when we were asked to pose for this photograph down at Streeter's Jetty, c1958.

Photographic Acknowledgements

Many of the photographs that appear in *Once in Broome* are from the private collection of the author. Special thanks to Pearl Hamaguchi, Honor Bin Salleh and Owen Torres for granting permission to reproduce photographs from their collections; and to Susan Sickert, Liz Janney (Broome Historical Society), and Linda Davis (The Battye Library) for their support in sourcing photographs.

Kind permission has also been received from the Broome Historical Society, The Battye Library, and the National Archives of Australia. Photographs from these collections appear as follows:

The Battye Library - 010855D Beagle Bay Church (exterior); 006952D Girl ironing; 022592PD Dutch war cemetery, 1948; 006950D Women fishing, 1953; 009060D Lorenzo gathering fish in his trap; 010835D At the pictures, Broome (inside), 1953; 011414D Nth side of Carnarvon Street; 000106D Broome cemetery; 010844D Girls at gymnasium, 1953; 010842D Boys at gymnasium, 1953.

Broome Historical Society - BM2006/823 Beagle Bay Church (interior); BM2006/944 Chinatown streetsign; BM2006/2004 Boy with bananas; BM2006/1353 Sun Pictures; BM2006/1054A Shiba Lane; BM2006/48 Streeter & Male.

National Archives of Australia - A1200, L15302 Cable Beach 1953; Old house near Broome airport K273/44 1937/11, part 1, photo 4, box 37; A1200, L11701 Pearling luggers, Roebuck Bay, 1949.